The Four Pillars of Spiritual Transformation

The Real God only reveals Himself to one who can no longer be described or named at all.

Muḥyiddīn Ibn ʿArabī

MYSTICAL TREATISES OF
MUHYIDDIN IBN ʿARABI

ALREADY AVAILABLE

The Universal Tree and the Four Birds
(*al-Ittiḥād al-kawnī*)

FORTHCOMING TITLES

The Book of Journeying
(*Kitāb al-isfār ʿan natāʾij al-asfār*)

Annihilated in Contemplation
(*Kitāb al-fanāʾ fiʾl-mushāhada*)

Technical Terms of Sufism
(*al-Iṣṭilāḥāt al-ṣūfīya*)

Muḥyiddīn Ibn ʿArabī

The Four Pillars of Spiritual Transformation

The Adornment of the Spiritually Transformed
(*Ḥilyat al-abdāl*)

Introduction, translation, and Arabic edition

STEPHEN HIRTENSTEIN

ANQA PUBLISHING • OXFORD

IN ASSOCIATION WITH THE
MUHYIDDIN IBN ʿARABI SOCIETY

Published by Anqa Publishing
PO Box 1178
Oxford OX2 8YS, UK
www.anqa.co.uk

In association with the
Muhyiddin Ibn ʿArabi Society
www.ibnarabisociety.org

First published 2008
Reprinted with amendments, 2014

Cover design: Michael Tiernan

Manuscript on the back cover: first page of Yusuf Ağa 4868,
copied in Malatya in AH 602.

British Library Cataloguing in Publication Data.
A catalogue record for this book is available from the British Library.

ISBN: 978 1 9059370 4 2

Printed and bound in the USA by
Edwards Brothers Inc.

CONTENTS

ACKNOWLEDGEMENTS

I owe special thanks to all the members and fellows of the Muhyiddin Ibn ʿArabi Society, especially those involved directly or indirectly in the Archiving Project, without whose generous support this would never have been completed. In addition, I am as ever extremely grateful to the staff in various Turkish manuscript libraries, in particular the director of the Bolge Library in Konya, Bekir Şahin, whose passion for preserving precious manuscripts and their contents knows no bounds. Thanks also to Richard and Karen Holding, Martin Notcutt and Deborah Freeman, who all participated in a dramatic rescue mission, to Nermine Hanno for inestimable help with the Arabic text, to Suha Taji-Farouki for her insightful comments and suggestions on the text and translation, and to Michael Tiernan for his unobtrusively efficient copyediting and typesetting skills.

INTRODUCTION

The way of the Lord and the way of the soul

The wise make spiritual discipline, abandonment of this world and other such things the primary condition for their thoughts to be free enough to receive spiritual matters. For spiritual things do not impart their effects unless the place [of reception] is emptied, made ready and turned towards their standpoint of view. Those who know God know that the relationship of all things to God is [but] one single relation. Thus they witness Him in everything and nothing veils them from Him.[1]

When Ibn ʿArabī began to devote himself in earnest to the spiritual Way in the year 580/1184, he frequented several different spiritual masters in Seville. Amongst them were a number who had been disciples of Ibn Mujāhid,[2] one of the most famous Sufis of the day. Ibn Mujāhid's creed was based upon the following *ḥadīth* of the Prophet: "Reckon with yourselves before you are brought to the Reckoning (on the Day of Judgment)."

> He would make a note of all his thoughts, actions, words, what he had heard and similar things. After the prayer of nightfall he would seclude himself in his room and go over all his actions of that day that demanded repentance and repented of them. He would do likewise with all that called for his gratitude. He would then compare his actions with what was required of him by the Sacred Law. Having done this he would sleep a little, after which he would rise to say his litanies (*wird*) and pray in accordance

1. *K. al-Wasāʾil al-sāʾil*, the words of Ibn ʿArabī according to his close disciple, Ibn Sawdakīn, p.22.

2. He died in 1178, when Ibn ʿArabi was only 13, and so it is quite possible that they hardly ever met in person.

with the custom of the Prophet. Thus he would sleep and pray alternately throughout the night.[3]

According to Ibn ʿArabī, this shaykh was once visited by the Almohad Sultan, Abu Yaʿqub, who asked him whether he ever felt lonely living on his own. He replied: "Intimacy with God abolishes all loneliness – how can I be alone when He is always present with me?" Ibn ʿArabī himself followed Ibn Mujāhid's teachings on self-discipline, and states that he benefited immensely from those who had been taught by him.

Modern times seem to have little in common with the simplicity of this kind of medieval world, where extremes of asceticism were commonly practised. Yet in all true spiritual traditions rigorous self-discipline is part of the training, be it by way of retreats, fasts or other kinds of abstentions. The value of such self-discipline lies solely in it being directed towards an aim: Reality alone, as It is in Itself. It is clear that in the case of Ibn Mujāhid, for example, his whole approach was dictated by love of God, his desire to conform as closely as possible to the Divine Will and to follow the model of the Prophet Muhammad. In Ibn ʿArabī's case, too, critical self-examination was subsumed within complete devotion to, and remembrance of, God. His focus was always, unwaveringly, God's Unity and incessant Self-Revelation.

Like all great masters of spirituality, Ibn ʿArabī delineates two fundamental and complementary facets of the Way: on the one hand, the belief in and knowledge of how things are in reality, based on the premise of God's Unity, and the ways that He has revealed Himself from time immemorial – the destination and aim; and on the other hand, the practice, the means of achieving the aim, which starts from where each person finds themselves, ignorant of reality, not yet having arrived. Writers from all traditions have spoken of the myriad pitfalls of the spiritual quest, and have laid out a programme for their

3. Austin, *Sufis of Andalusia*, p.146, from the *Durrat al-Fākhira* (MS. Esad Ef. 1777).

disciples involving stages and states that must be passed through if one is to reach the reality of the Divine Beloved. Ibn ʿArabī's "spiritual method" tends to be built more upon dialectic and paradox. For example, his attitude is revealed in the way he speaks of an encounter with two of his masters in al-Andalus during his youth:

> I was once in Seville with my master Abū al-ʿAbbās al-ʿUryānī and he said to me: "My son, concern yourself with your Lord!" I left his house exhilarated, reeling under the effect of the teaching he had given me. I then went to see my master Abū ʿImrān Mūsā b. ʿImrān al-Martulī in his mosque (where he was imam), which was called the Mosque of al-Rida. I greeted him and he welcomed me, and then he said: "My son, concern yourself with your soul (*nafs*)!" So I said to him: "Master, you have told me to concern myself with my soul, while our master Ahmad [al-ʿUryānī] told me: "Concern yourself with your Lord." What am I to do?" He replied: "My son, each of us instructs you according to the requirements of his own spiritual state, but what the master Abū al-ʿAbbās has indicated to you is preferable, and may God grant us that!" Then I went back to al-ʿUryānī and told him what had happened. He said to me: "My dear child, both points of view are correct: Abū ʿImrān has spoken to you about the beginning and the way to follow (*ṭarīq*), while I have drawn your attention to the final end of the quest (the Divine Companion who is ever-present, *rafīq*), so that when you follow the way your spiritual aspiration will be raised higher than that which is other than God."[4]

This dual approach is very characteristic of Ibn ʿArabī's teaching, and he plays with the two rhyming terms Spiritual Way (*ṭarīq*) and Divine Companion (*rafīq*) to show that they are inextricably linked. God is simultaneously ever-present and the end-point of the

4. *The Brilliant Star in the life of Dhu'l-Nun the Egyptian* (*al-Kawkab al-durrī fī manāqib Dhī'l-Nūn al-Miṣrī*), translated into French by Roger Deladrière as *La Vie merveilleuse de Dhū l-Nūn l'Égyptien*, p. 161.

spiritual journey. Even though we may be full of internal chatter and gossip, lost in the crowd of states, filled with insatiable wants, asleep and forgetful of our real nature, there is always the spark of new life from the One "who is closer to [man] than his jugular vein" (Q.50.16). For Ibn 'Arabī, the desire to turn away from normal gratifications towards the Truth Itself is already a response, because we are desired; we only seek because we are sought. As he succinctly exhorts his reader elsewhere,

> Therefore, my brother, follow this Path and say "the Companion, the Companion", so that you can join with Him without any separation, and separate from Him without any connection, and your shadows will always bow down to Him, morning and evening![5]

The writing of the Ḥilyat al-abdāl

The *Ḥilyat al-abdāl* must rank as one of the most popular short treatises written by Ibn 'Arabī, as attested by the many copies to be found in manuscript libraries throughout the world. Its enduring popularity may be due to the practical nature of the text, addressing the methodology of the spiritual Path in deep but accessible terms. As the author explains in his introduction to the work, it was written in response to a specific request made by two of his closest companions, Badr al-Ḥabashī and Muḥammad b. Khālid al-Ṣadafī, while he was in Mecca. They had asked him to write something for them "from which they could benefit concerning the Path of the hereafter (*ṭarīq al-ākhira*)".

The Meccan period of Ibn 'Arabī's life can be viewed as the fulcrum of his earthly existence. Born in Murcia in 560/1165, he spent some 36 years in the Muslim West, the Maghrib, and another 36 years in the Muslim East, the Mashriq, with about 3 years in Mecca

5. *The Fabulous Gryphon* (*'Anqā' Mughrib*), translated by Gerald Elmore as *Islamic Sainthood in the Fullness of Time*, p.255.

in between. This three-year period both connects and differentiates the two halves of Ibn ʿArabī's life. To give some idea of how cataclysmic his Meccan period was, let us recall how it was in Mecca that he met the Youth with no name, through whose silent instruction he began the writing of the enormous *Futūḥāt al-Makkīya*;[6] it was in Mecca that his status as Seal of Muhammadian Sainthood was confirmed in a glorious vision of the Prophet;[7] it was in Mecca that he had the dream of the two bricks and his encounter with the Kaʿba;[8] it was in Mecca that love of women was first evoked in his heart by the beautiful Niẓām, source of the inspiration for his wonderful collection of poems, the *Tarjumān al-ashwāq*;[9] and it was in Mecca that he first savoured the pleasures of married life, marrying and becoming a father.[10] His literary output during this time was also prodigious: apart from the first chapters of the *Futūḥāt*, he composed the *Rūḥ al-quds* (which includes stories of the saintly men and women he had known in the Maghrib),[11] the *Mishkāt al-anwār* (one of the first written collections of *ḥadīth qudsī*),[12] the *Tāj al-Rasā'il* (a collection of eight love-letters to the Kaʿba) and the *Ḥilyat al-abdāl*.

The *Ḥilyat al-abdāl* was written in the year 599 / January 1203 in Tā'if in the space of an hour,[13] while on a visit to the tomb of the Prophet's cousin, ʿAbd Allāh Ibn ʿAbbās. Ibn ʿAbbās is one of

6. See *al-Futūḥāt al-Makkīya*, I.47ff., translated in Hirtenstein, *Unlimited Mercifier*, p. 151.

7. It appears in the Preface to the *Futūḥāt* itself (*Fut*.I.3). See Hirtenstein, *Unlimited Mercifier*, pp. 152–3.

8. *Fut*.I.319, and Hirtenstein, *Unlimited Mercifier*, p. 154.

9. See *Tarjumān al-ashwāq* (translated by Reynold Nicholson), p. 14, and Hirtenstein, *Unlimited Mercifier*, p. 148.

10. His first wife was Fātima b. Yūnus, and their first son Muḥammad ʿImāduddīn was almost certainly born in Mecca. See ibid., p. 150.

11. The autobiographical section has been translated by Ralph Austin in *Sufis of Andalusia*.

12. Translated as *Divine Sayings* by Stephen Hirtenstein and Martin Notcutt.

13. The timing is specified in his *Fihrist* (MS. Yusuf Ağa 7838, fol. 190b). Tā'if is a city some two days' journey from Mecca, known as the garden of the Hijaz because of its good climate and green fields.

the great figures of early Islam: blessed with a prodigious memory and great insight, he was famed for his interpretation of the Quran. Ibn ʿArabī refers to him as one of the elite group of saints known as the singulars (*afrād*). He also quotes Ibn ʿAbbās's comment on a particular verse in the Quran regarding the seven heavens[14]: "If I were to explain its true meaning, you would stone me for being an unbeliever" – as we shall see later, the mention of the heavens is not so unconnected or insignificant in connection with the particular kind of saints known as *abdāl* (the Substitutes or the Spiritually Transformed). Just as Ibn ʿAbbās expounded the meanings of the revelation of the Quran, so Ibn ʿArabī in this treatise explains the meaning behind a revelatory incident drawn from his own experience. It is therefore fitting that at Ibn ʿAbbās's resting-place Ibn ʿArabī should have been inspired to expound upon the spiritual discipline that truly frees man into a different world, and those who are masters of it.

In his introduction Ibn ʿArabī explains the reason behind his writing of this treatise: "I have written this booklet [for my companions] and entitled it: 'The Adornment of the Spiritually Transformed and those spiritual knowledges and states that manifest from it' (*Ḥilyat al-abdāl wa mā yaẓharu ʿanhā min al-maʿārif wa al-aḥwāl*), that it may be for them and others of some assistance upon the Path to true happiness."

The Spiritually Transformed Saints (abdāl)

The *abdāl* (sing. *badal*, lit. "substitutes" or "successors", but can also mean "generous" and "noble") are a special category of saint mentioned by the Prophet Muhammad in various accounts. Many of these are apparently contradictory. For example, Muhammad

14. "He who created the seven heavens and likewise of the earth, His order descends amongst them" (Q.65.12), quoted in Ibn ʿArabī's *K. al-Fanā' fī al-mushāhada*, translated by Stephen Hirtenstein and Layla Shamash.

is reported to have said that the *abdāl* in his community number 30 and are similar to the Prophet Abraham (Ibn ʿAsākir, 1/60–1), while according to another report, which ʿAlī b. Abī Ṭālib quotes in response to being urged to curse the people of Syria, "the *abdāl* are in al-Shām (Greater Syria) and they number 40 men; whenever one of them dies, God substitutes him with another. By means of them God brings down the rain, gives victory over their enemies, and averts punishment from the people of al-Shām" (Ibn Ḥanbal, 1/112; Ibn ʿAsākir, 1/60). Even to this day there is a special site associated with the *abdāl* in Damascus, the so-called "Cave of the Forty", where the replacement of one saint by another is reputed to take place.

In Sufi literature there are also marked differences in the way the term is used and understood. Most authors consider them, on the basis of a *ḥadīth*, as part of the hierarchy of saints, whose total number they take to be 356 (300 on the heart of Adam, 40 on the heart of Noah or Moses, 7 on the heart of Abraham, 5 on the heart of Gabriel, 3 on the heart of Michael and finally 1 on the heart of Seraphiel). Ibn ʿArabī, on the other hand, while agreeing with this perspective from one point of view, adds that through unveiling he has been shown that the total number of saints is 589 (all of whom, apart from the Muhammadian Seal, are to be found in every age).[15]

The early Sufis tended to stress the visible acts which the *abdāl* performed. Thus, according to Abū Ṭālib al-Makkī, they are characterized by satisfaction with God, compassion towards His creatures, purity of heart and the ability to give wise counsel to the community.[16] ʿAbd Allāh Anṣārī states that they avoid killing living creatures and are capable of miraculous acts of grace (*karāmāt*), without falling prey to self-deception or pride.[17]

15. For further details, see Chodkiewicz, *Seal of the Saints*, pp. 53ff., and *Fut.*II.40–1.
16. See *Qūt al-qulūb*, 2/78.
17. See *Ṭabaqāt al-ṣūfiya*, pp. 415, 513 and 611.

The abdāl according to Ibn 'Arabī

In Ibn 'Arabī's writings there are many different kinds of saint (*walī*). What they all have in common is the fact that they "have been taken charge of (*tawallā*) by God, by His helping them in their struggles against the four enemies: the passions (*hawā*), the self (*nafs*), the world (*dunyā*) and the devil (*shayṭān*); and the knowledge of these pillars (*arkān*) is the knowledge spoken of by al-Muḥāsibī".[18]

Ibn 'Arabī provides us with a much more detailed picture of the *abdāl*, their place within the saintly hierarchy, their functions and their relationship to the Divine Names. He tells us there are seven *abdāl* at any one time.[19] They are under the jurisdiction of the Pole (*quṭb*), and have the power to break through the normal bounds of time and space by appearing in two places simultaneously. At the same time the term can sometimes be used to refer to the elite group of saints: the Pole, the two Imams and the four Supports (*awtād*), although more commonly he uses it to designate a further category since the Supports are made up of the Pole and the two Imams (see below on letters).

He relates the seven *abdāl* to other sevens. Firstly, each is responsible for a different "clime" (*iqlīm*) or terrestrial region. The idea of "clime" was inherited from the Greek tradition (Gk, κλίμα), and was used to describe a zone extending in longitude from one edge of the inhabited world to the other, situated between two lines of latitude.

18. *Fut.*II.53. Abū 'Abd Allāh al-Ḥārith al-Muḥāsibī (d. 243/857) was a famous Shafi'i jurist and theologian in Baghdad, renowned for his mystical writings and as the teacher of Junayd. He was nicknamed al-Muḥāsibī after his scrupulous practice of introspective self-examination (*muḥāsaba*). His most influential work was *Kitāb al-Ri'āya li-ḥuqūq Allāh* (The Book of Observance concerning the Rights of God). Ibn 'Arabi commented on his *Sharḥ al-ma'rifa* in front of a great spiritual master, Ibn Ja'dūn of Fez (see Austin, *Sufis of Andalusia*, p. 115).

19. Later he appears to contradict this by saying there are also 40 or 12 (also called *nuqabā'*), but this may be a device to prevent the mind of the reader from fixing the saintly hierarchy into some sort of intellectual system – see *Fut.*II.5–16.

Traditionally there were said to be seven (although some Arab writers increased these to 14 or 16), and each zone was also conceived of as being under the rulership of one of the seven known planetary bodies.

Each of the *abdāl* therefore derives his terrestrial responsibility from walking in the footsteps of a prophet, not as a temporal figure but as the spiritual reality who has jurisdiction over one of the seven planetary heavens. Just as each clime is under a particular planet, so each *badal* is under the prophetic reality of a particular heaven. These are the seven heavens of the ascension (*mi'rāj*), upon which the Prophet Muhammad was taken by Gabriel and which is accomplished spiritually by his heirs.[20] We may summarize his exposition in the following table:

Abdāl	**In the footsteps of**	**Heaven**	**Planet**
1.	Abraham (Ibrāhīm)	7th	Saturn
2.	Moses (Mūsā)	6th	Jupiter
3.	Aaron (Hārūn)	5th	Mars
4.	Enoch (Idrīs)	4th	Sun
5.	Joseph (Yūsuf)	3rd	Venus
6.	Jesus ('Īsā)	2nd	Mercury
7.	Adam	1st	Moon

He also mentions that John the Baptist (Yaḥyā) participates in two of these heavens, alternating between Aaron and Jesus. To the hearts of the seven *abdāl* are revealed some of the realities of these prophets and the secrets and mysteries of their planetary spheres.[21]

20. The ascension theme is a central one which Ibn 'Arabī treats in many different ways: notably, the *K. al-Isrā'*, where he describes his own great ascension in highly poetic and allusive terms, the *R. al-Anwār* and Chapters 167 and 367 in the *Futūḥāt*.

21. For further details of these and other correspondences, see *The Seven Days of*

In addition, each *badal* is attached as servant to a particular Divine Name, through which God observes the person and which is dominant over them. These Names, which are known as the seven Divine Attributes, the fundamental principles of all manifestation, govern the *abdāl* so that each *badal* is known as:

1. ʿAbd al-Ḥayy (Living)
2. ʿAbd al-ʿAlīm (Knowing)
3. ʿAbd al-Murīd/Wadūd (Desiring/Ever-Loving)[22]
4. ʿAbd al-Qādir (Powerful/Able)[23]
5. ʿAbd al-Shakūr (Grateful)[24]
6. ʿAbd al-Samīʿ (Hearing)
7. ʿAbd al-Baṣīr (Seeing)

Although Ibn ʿArabī does not specify which Name belongs to which *badal*, leaving his schema somewhat open to the insight of his readers, elsewhere in the *Futūḥāt* he correlates these Divine Names to specific days of the week, and therefore implicitly to the prophetic realities who rule them and the *abdāl* who represent them. He states that the movement of each day comes from one of the Divine Attributes, as follows:

---

the Heart, a translation of Ibn ʿArabī's *Awrād* by Pablo Beneito and Stephen Hirtenstein, pp. 11–15 and Appendix A.

22. The Name *Murīd* is specified in the first version of the *Futūḥāt*, while the second version gives the Name *Wadūd* here, referring specifically to the quality of Love that pervades creation and thus the creature. While it is identical to the original Divine Desire to be known, nonetheless the servant who is under this quality is more linked to its expression in the world as Love.

23. The author says that the first four Names (*Ḥayy*, *ʿAlīm*, *Murīd* and *Qādir*) are also those of the four *awtād*. Thus the Name *Ḥayy* (Living) acts like the Pole amongst the Names, since all things are imbued with this essential quality.

24. This is more traditionally referred to as *al-Mutakallim* (Speaking), but here Ibn ʿArabī seems to be emphasizing the act of giving thanks on the part of the creature rather than the existentiating command 'Be' of the Divine.

- Sunday (day of Enoch/Idrīs): Hearing, since there is nothing in the world that does not hear the Divine Command 'Be' (*kun*) in the state of its non-existence
- Monday (day of Adam): Life, as there is no part of the world that is not alive
- Tuesday (day of Aaron): Seeing, since everything witnesses its Creator
- Wednesday (day of Jesus): Will, as all things endeavour to glorify the One who gave them existence
- Thursday (day of Moses): Power, since there is nothing in existence that is not able to repeat the praises (*thanā'*) of the Creator
- Friday (day of Joseph): Knowledge, as there is no part of the world that does not know its Creator by virtue of its own self
- Saturday (day of Abraham): Speaking, since all things are speaking in praise (*ḥamd*) of their Creator

We may also note here that these "days" represent the order of creation as experienced by each creature, from the state of non-existence to the state of worldly existence.[25]

Furthermore, he records elsewhere[26] that each *badal* possesses a verse from the Quran which functions as his sacred privilege or contemplative mode of being (*ḥijjīr*) and spiritual station (*maqām*). These seven verses, which indicate successive degrees of contemplation and realization, summarize the stages in the coming-into-being of the fully Human Being (*insān*):

1. "There is nothing like His Likeness" (Q.42.11)
2. "The seas would run out before the Words of my Lord are exhausted" (Q.18.109)

25. *Fut*.II.438. For further details, see Mohamed Haj Yousef, *Ibn ʿArabî: Time and Cosmology*, pp. 52 and 109.

26. See *Fut*.I.156, from Chapter 15 on the "spiritual knowledge of the breaths and the knowledge of their Poles who are realized in them and their secrets".

3. "[in the earth are Signs for those of sure faith] and within yourselves, do you then not see?" (Q.51.21)
4. "O would that I were dust!" (Q.78.40)
5. "Question the people of remembrance if it should be that you do not know" (Q.16.43)
6. "I commit my affair to God" (Q.40.44)
7. "We offered the trust [to the heavens and the earth and the mountains, but they refused to carry it and were afraid of it; and man carried it]" (Q.33.72)

Only with the realization of the seventh degree of the Divine "trust" (*amāna*) is the real rank of Adamic Man reached, in which the human being can truly be said to be created in the Divine image.

In yet another mode of expressing this sevenfold mystery, Ibn 'Arabī describes seven of the letters of the Arabic alphabet as the equivalent of the *abdāl*. As Denis Gril has remarked, "the letters, like Man, receive the Divine Discourse. They are thus capable of expressing all realities (*ḥaqā'iq*), especially those realities that make up the human world. Their order follows a hierarchy similar to that of the Initiates."[27] Thus the *alif* stands for the Pole (*quṭb*), the *wāw* and *yā'* for the two Imams, the *nūn* for the fourth Support (*watad*), and these four letters plus *tā'*, *kāf* and *hā'* equate to the seven *abdāl*. The first three letters and their vowel equivalents (a, u and i) with the *nūn* are the signs of Arabic syntax, with all its movements through case endings, conjugation and number. The final three letters specifically represent the verb's pronominal suffixes, i.e. the substitution of one person for another (I, you, he/she): for Ibn 'Arabī these are not simply different persons as such, but rather the various aspects of one person seen from different points of view. This helps to explain the essential principle of interchangeability among the human *abdāl*.

Ibn 'Arabī says that the reason the *abdāl* are known as such is due to their peculiar ability to appear in two places at one and the same

27. *The Meccan Revelations* (ed. Michel Chodkiewicz), Vol. II, pp. 118ff.

time, leaving a "substitute" (*badal*) in their own house who interacts with others as necessary, without those people ever knowing that it is not the actual person himself they are talking to. He derives this meaning from the root of the word (*b-d-l*, "to change the semblance of something" or "to substitute one thing for another"), and seems to have in mind some of its Quranic associations: for example, "God will change their evil deeds by substituting for them good deeds" (Q.25.70). But for him this is not simply a linguistic fancy in its application to human substitution, but a matter of actual direct experience, both for himself and other people that he knew.

Ibn ʿArabī's meetings with the abdāl

While in Mecca he had a dramatic meeting with a group of unnamed saints whom he simply refers to as "the Seven Persons":

> I met them at a spot between the wall of the Hanbalites and the bench of Zamzam. They were truly the elect of God. They never blinked their eyes at all, being under the dominion of holy Tranquillity and Awe. When I met them, they were in a state of pure contemplation, so no word passed between me and them on any matter of knowledge, but I saw in them an almost unimaginable calm and repose."[28]

Elsewhere he identifies them as the *abdāl* who are mentioned in this treatise, saying: "We saw these seven *abdāl* in Mecca: we came across them behind the wall of the Hanbalites, and joined them there – I have never seen anyone with more beautiful qualities than them."[29] Although he does not specify exactly when this meeting took place, it may well have occurred just before or after the writing of this treatise on the *abdāl*.

28. *Rūh al-quds* (ed. Mahmud Ghorab), p.130; Austin, *Sufis of Andalusia*, pp.141–2.
29. *Fut.*II.8. See also *Fut.*II.455, translated in *Quest for the Red Sulphur* by Claude Addas, p.216.

He also relates how he himself met one of the *abdāl* called Mūsā Abū ʿImrān al-Sadrānī in 586/1189 in a remarkable encounter that broke the rules of normal space, allowing apparently instantaneous translocation: he had just performed the sunset prayer at his house in Seville, and suddenly conceived an extremely strong desire to see the great Maghribi master Abū Madyan, who lived in Bijāya (in modern Algeria, some 45 days' journey away).

> After the sunset prayer I performed two cycles of the supererogatory prayer, and as I was saying the ritual greeting (*taslīm*), Abū ʿImrān came in and greeted me. I sat him down next to me and enquired where he had come from, to which he replied that he had come from Abū Madyan at Bijāya. Upon my asking him when he had been with him, he replied that he had only just finished praying the sunset prayer with him. He told me that Abū Madyan had said to him, "Certain things have occurred to the mind of Muḥammad b. al-ʿArabī in Seville, so go at once and answer him on my behalf."[30]

Apart from his own personal meetings with such saints, he also relates three incidents regarding other people that he personally knew and one of the *abdāl*: one as part of this treatise, which involved one of his companions in al-Andalus (see below, pp. 31–2, 43), and twice in his *Futūḥāt*. The *Futūḥāt* meetings shed further light on the elevated degree of these men of God, who exhibit apparently miraculous powers:

> I once met one of the wandering pilgrims on the sea-coast between Marsā Laqīṭ and the light-house [near Tunis]. He told me that on the same spot he had come across one of the *abdāl* walking upon

30. He goes on to recount how Abū Madyan told him via this companion Mūsā al-Sadrānī that they were destined never to meet physically in the world although this would not affect their meeting spiritually (*Rūḥ al-quds*, pp. 74–6; Austin, *Sufis of Andalusia*, pp. 121–3). In addition, Ibn ʿArabī names two other people he knew as *abdāl*: Muḥammad b. Ashraf al-Rundī, the remarkable saint of Ronda (*Rūḥ al-quds*, pp. 72–4; Austin, *Sufis of Andalusia*, pp. 116–21), and a man considered by others to be one of the *abdāl*, Yūsuf b. Sakhr in Cordoba (ibid., p. 159).

the waves of the sea. He said: "I greeted him and he returned my greeting. This was a time of great injustice and oppression in the country, so I asked him what he thought of all the terrible things that were happening in the country. He glared at me angrily and said: 'What is that to you or to God's servants? Don't speak of anything but that which is good! May God grant you help and accept your apology for this.'"[31]

In Chapter 8 of his *Futūḥāt*, Ibn ʿArabī recounts a tale involving one of his "eastern" companions and friends, Awḥad al-dīn Ḥāmid b. Abī al-Fakhr al-Kirmānī. This story seems to be the experiential confirmation of Ibn ʿArabī's doctrine of human "substitution". When he was a young man, al-Kirmānī had been in the service of a shaykh who had fallen ill. On arriving in Tikrīt (in modern Iraq), he asked permission from his master to go and get some medicine for him from the head of the Sanjar hospital who happened to be there. With his shaykh's authorization he went at night to the official's tent, which was full of people: on seeing him, the hospital head got up to meet him, even though apparently he was unknown to him, and asked the young man what he wanted. When he heard the news of al-Kirmanī's master, the official had the medicine brought for him and accompanied him outside the tent, with a candle. When the young man got back to his shaykh, he recounted the remarkably kind reception he had received from this dignitary, at which his master smiled and said:

> My dear child, I was inspired by my concern for you. Seeing how sorry you were for me, I let you do what you asked. But when you were gone, I was afraid that the amīr[32] would put you to shame

31. *Fut.*I.707. Marsā Laqīt is a coastal village to the north-west of Tunis, home of Ibn ʿArabī's teacher al-Kinānī. The light-house is where his friend and teacher, ʿAbd al-ʿAzīz al-Mahdawī, lived and had a group of students. Ibn ʿArabi spent time with both these masters when he stayed in Tunis – see Hirtenstein, *Unlimited Mercifier*, pp.87–9 and 144–6.

32. Literally, prince or commander, but here the term refers rather to the high official status of the hospital head.

> by refusing to receive you. So I separated myself from my own corporeal habitation (*haykal*); I entered that of the amīr and sat down in his place. When you arrived, it was I who greeted you and behaved towards you as you saw. Then I returned to this habitation of mine. As a matter of fact, I don't need this drug and have no use for it.[33]

Ibn ʿArabī adds: "So this person had manifested in the form of someone else."

Bearing in mind the exalted degree of sainthood which is manifested in these "Substitutes", this book of the *Ḥilyat al-abdāl* focuses more on how they attain to their special transformed state. The *abdāl*, for Ibn ʿArabī, is a coded reference to people who have gone far beyond the confines of earthly existence, who have realized the spiritual and divine dimension of their being, whose spiritual ascension has transformed them. They not only represent the accomplishment of the ascension, the fact that it can be done; they are also the embodiment of this possibility inherent in any human being. Therefore how they achieve this condition is of paramount importance to others.

The title: Ḥilyat al-abdāl

Anyone familiar with Arabic hagiography will immediately find an echo of the title of the voluminous work by Ibn ʿArabī's predecessor, Abu Nuʿaym al-Isfahānī (d. 430/1038), the *Ḥilyat al-awliyā'* ("The Adornment of the Friends of God"). Given that Abū Nuʿaym's work abounds with tales of saints from the first two centuries of Islam, one might be disappointed to find that this treatise by Ibn ʿArabī contains no such stories of saintly men and women, apart from a brief biographical anecdote regarding a friend in al-Andalus, which acts as his contemplative starting-point. The text here is designed,

33. *Fut.*I.127, translated by Henry Corbin in *Spiritual Body and Celestial Earth*, p. 140.

rather, to give direct practical advice to those striving on the spiritual Path.

The original meaning of *ḥilyat* (adornment) can be found in the Quran, in relation to the Divine gift: "He it is who has made subservient the sea, that you might eat from it fresh food and take from it ornaments (*ḥilyat*) to wear."[34] However, when applied to the human being, the term came to signify the qualities, condition or appearance of the person. It particularly refers to the exterior or visible qualities of a man (in contrast to the ornamentation and jewellery that embellishes a woman). It is related etymologically to the word *taḥallī* (having the qualities of), a term which is very specific in Ibn ʿArabī's terminology:

> It is being qualified by the Divine characteristics, which is expressed in the spiritual Path as being endowed with the traits (*takhalluq*) of the Names. According to us, *taḥallī* is always the appearance of the characteristics of true servanthood to God (*ʿubūda*), despite being endowed with the traits of the [Divine] Names ... The qualification of the servant with the characteristics of true servanthood is part of his being qualified with the Divine characteristics, but most people do not understand this.[35]

Thus for Ibn ʿArabī the emphasis should be upon the perfect balance between the human as "servant", as a pure place of reception for the Divine that acts within him, and the human reality as image of God. Just as the image in the mirror reflects the onlooker but has no reality of its own, so nothing really belongs to the pure servant who is the place of God's manifestation: he is empty of self-existence, quality or act, thus allowing the complete Divine Image, which is the total of the Divine Names, to manifest through him. He knows himself, as this treatise mentions, to be "one who can no longer be described or named at all".

34. Q.16.14. See also Q.35.12.

35. *Fut.*II.128 (Ch. 73, q.153). Here Ibn ʿArabī also defines *ʿubūda* as the relation of the servant to God, not to his own soul (the latter being technically *ʿubūdīya*).

The focus of the *Ḥilyat al-abdāl*, as Ibn ʿArabī makes clear, is on how the *abdāl* become *abdāl*, or the spiritual deeds that adorn them. In other words, it concerns the prerequisites and visible qualities for this condition of "emptiness". In this sense it is an intensely practical work, and one which should be of value to anyone with spiritual aspirations.

The structure of the Ḥilyat al-abdāl

In conformity to the notion of seven *abdāl*, there are seven sections delineated in the work.

1. In the first, which mentions the writing of the text in response to the request of his two companions, Badr al-Ḥabashī and Muḥammad al-Ṣadafī, Ibn ʿArabī alludes to the contents by stating that this is "a chapter that brings together the various forms of spiritual desire (*irāda*)". For Ibn ʿArabī the term *irāda* signifies a yearning in the heart, which he distinguishes elsewhere in two ways: a natural yearning which includes some kind of self-gratification; and the desire for the Real, which is founded on unconditioned purity (*ikhlāṣ*).[36] It is this latter kind which forms the subject-matter of the treatise.

2. The second section then describes "the various forms of spiritual desire", which constitute four basic conditions of the spiritual life: renunciation (giving up the pleasures of this world for the recompense of the next); trust (handing over one's affairs and choice to

36. See Ibn ʿArabī's *al-Iṣṭilāḥāt al-ṣūfīya*, no. 2 (*irāda*) (critical edition forthcoming). Real desire or yearning can be seen in the following prayer: "You are the One who accomplishes whatever You desire, while I am a servant for You, one among several of the servants. O My God, You have desired me and You have desired of me – thus I am the desired and You are the Desirer. May You be what is desired of me, so that You [Yourself] become the Desired and I the desirer" (from the Thursday morning prayer in Ibn ʿArabī's *Awrād*, see Beneito and Hirtenstein, *Seven Days of the Heart*, p. 102).

the Lord); aspiration (for states of closeness to God); and worship (devoting oneself to Him and striving). Yet in all these cases there is still the illusion of self-existence: "the renunciate", he says, "abandons the world in order to be recompensed ... the worshipper strives hard because he longs for closeness" and so on. Each of these aspects demonstrates the taint of an individual self-willed choice, inevitably at variance with the sheer Divine purity, which the Prophet Muhammad referred to as "God is and there is not with Him a thing". These four types are summarized as "aspirants" (*murīdūn*), and form the first group of people described in this treatise.

Beyond these, he describes two other categories, where the human has been completely taken out of his own action or will. These are described as the people of the letter *Bā'* and the people of the letter *Lām*: the first Ibn 'Arabī calls people of wisdom and gnosis, who know that God is the tongue by which they praise Him, the hand with which they take and so on;[37] the second are people of authority and true knowledge, who know that God praises Himself by their tongue, that God Himself takes with their hand and so on. Unlike others who believe that they praise God by their own selves, both these groups have realized servanthood, their utter indigence before God, but it is only the second, the people of *Lām*, who have penetrated to the fullest condition of realization – for they have relinquished the illusion of possessing not just their qualities and powers but even their very selfhood. They know who and what they truly are. Both groups are known as "verifiers" (*muḥaqqiqūn*), those who have realized the interior meaning of things, people of the inner heart, and they form the second group referred to in the treatise.

This section is completed by a four-line poem, hinting that the treatise was composed in a vision of clear insight (*bayyina*) and a Divine "Address" (*khiṭāb*).

37. As in the *ḥadīth*: "My servant does not cease to draw close to Me with supererogatory works until I love him; and when I love him, I become his hearing by which he hears, his seeing by which he sees, his hand with which he takes, his foot with which he walks."

3. In the third section Ibn ʿArabī recounts an episode from his youth in al-Andalus, where one of his companions encountered one of the *abdāl*. During their rather shocking meeting in his house, Ibn ʿArabī's friend, ʿAbd al-Majīd b. Salama, is inspired to ask how the *abdāl* become *abdāl*, and is told that it is through four things: silence, seclusion, hunger and vigilance. These four are then described in the remaining sections of the treatise, which ends with a poem of exhortation to one who desires "the spiritual abodes of the Substitutes". Thus a personal anecdote is given universal significance.

The four pillars of knowledge

Ibn ʿArabī describes silence, seclusion, hunger and vigilance as the four pillars of spiritual knowledge (*arkān al-maʿrifa*). In describing them as 'pillars', Ibn ʿArabī is implying a direct equivalent or correspondence to the five Pillars of the Islamic religion (*arkān al-islām*), that is, the practices of the testimony of faith (*shahāda*), ritual prayer (*ṣalāt*), alms-giving (*zakāt*), fasting (*ṣawm*) and pilgrimage (*ḥajj*), the first equating to spiritual knowledge (*maʿrifa*). It is also in correspondence with his notion of "the pillars of the religion" (*arkān al-dīn*), which he mentions as faith (*īmān*), sainthood (*wilāya*), prophethood (*nubuwwa*) and envoyship (*risāla*). The same four principles are treated at greater length and from different perspectives in the *Futūḥāt*.[38] We have also provided a translation of Chapter 53 (Appendix A), where Ibn ʿArabī discusses what can be done by an aspirant prior to finding a true spiritual master, and where he also recounts the story of his Andalusian friend. This text provides an interesting complement to the *Ḥilyat al-abdāl*, treating

38. See Chapters 80 and 81 (seclusion and leaving seclusion), 96 and 97 (silence and speech), 98 and 99 (vigilance and sleep) and 106 and 107 (hunger and abandonment of hunger). These pairs which complement and oppose each other are striking examples of the non-stop movement through all the states and stations which Ibn ʿArabī propounds. See Michel Chodkiewicz, "*Mirʿāj al-kalima*", in *Reason and Inspiration* (ed. Todd Lawson).

the same themes in the context of nine spiritual principles. He mentions these four as some of the things to be practised so that one "becomes firmly established in the affirmation/realization of Unity (*tawḥīd*)". He describes two as actions of commission (hunger and seclusion) and two as actions of omission (vigilance and silence), and as in this treatise, points out that "hunger includes vigilance, and seclusion includes silence". Interestingly, he specifies that according to the people of God, seclusion is the "chief of the four".

Other chapters in the *Futūḥāt* provide more detail on the individual principles. Chapter 80, for example, discusses the nature of seclusion, stressing the internal meaning and therefore more universal nature of the principle.

> None is in seclusion except one who knows himself, and he who knows himself knows his Lord. He has no object of contemplation except God, by virtue of His Most Beautiful Names, and he is characterized by them in both his interior and exterior.[39]

Referring particularly to Divine Names that can have a negative connotation, e.g. the Proud (*mutakabbir*) and the One who enforces or compels (*jabbār*), "he secludes himself from the likeness of these Divine Names due to what they contain in terms of negative attribute if someone is named by them or manifests with their properties in the world. Man's reality is to be totally indigent, and one who is indigent cannot be self-important or proud."[40]

Yet further than this is the one who secludes himself from all the Divine Names, since they belong to God alone. Even though he may be dressed in the likeness of all the Names, yet he prefers to rest in poverty and indigence. Such a one returns to his native land, which is absolute servanthood, and this Ibn ʿArabī considers to be the real place of Man. He continues:

39. *Fut.*II.153, the beginning of Chapter 80 on seclusion.

40. Ibid.: here he mentions two verses in the Quran that specify the negative aspects of Divine Names when applied to the human being: "[Now] taste! Surely thou art the mighty one, the noble (*al-ʿazīz al-karīm*)" (Q.44.49) and "Thus does God set a seal upon every heart, self-important, haughty (*mutakabbir jabbār*)" (Q.40.35).

> The servant returns to his own special quality, which is utter servanthood (*'ubūda*) in which Lordship does not compete. He is adorned (*taḥallā*) by that, seated in the house of his potential reality, not his existence in Being.[41] He observes the dispensation of God within him, and he is secluded from spiritual directorship (*tadbīr*) in that.

Here again one may note how he makes a passing reference to what really constitutes the description of servanthood, i.e. adornment (*taḥallī*) – the use of such quite deliberate terminology provides links between apparently disparate texts.

In the *Ḥilyat al-abdāl* Ibn 'Arabī presents his teachings in a most succinct way. Describing the four pillars or rules in terms of how they are understood by the aspirant (*murīd*) and the verifier (*muḥaqqiq*), he speaks of them as a spiritual state (*ḥāl*) and a spiritual station (*maqām*) and as bearing fruit in a particular domain of spiritual knowledge (*ma'rifa*). We may tabulate his exposition in the diagram on the facing page.[42]

Were we to take them simply at face value, as practices, "things to be done", we would clearly miss the essential point which Ibn 'Arabī is making. All that is physical has its root in that which is spiritual: all our practice is preparation, to bring us to a point where one allows the acknowledgement of the Divine in all His fundamental and rightful height and glory, remaining in pure servanthood while He remains in full sovereignty.

What is absolutely remarkable about this masterwork is how precise and all-encompassing Ibn 'Arabī's descriptions of spiritual practice are: he gives us, in the space of a few pages, enough material to contemplate and act on for a lifetime. Whatever forms of spiritual practice we may come across, they are forms or effects of these four,

41. Literally: "the house of the thingness of his potentiality, not the thingness of his existence".

42. Slightly adapted from M. Vâlsan's introduction to his translation of the text, *La Parure des Abdāl*, p. 37.

The four pillars of knowledge

The four pillars (*arkān*)	Spiritual states		Spiritual stations and secrets (*maqāmāt/asrār*)	Domains of knowledge (*maʿārif*)
	For the aspirant (*murīd/sālik*)	For the verifier (*muḥaqqiq/muqarrab*)		
SILENCE (*ṣamt*)	Safety from harm	Intimate converse	Inspiration (*waḥy*)	God (*Allāh*)
SECLUSION (*ʿuzla*)	Transcendent of all attributes		Divine Unity (*waḥdāniyya*) Uniqueness [quality] (*aḥadiyya*)	This world (*dunyā*)
HUNGER (*jūʿ*)	Humility, submission, servility, lack of self-importance, calm, indigence, absence of base thoughts	Delicacy of feeling, serenity, intimacy, non-worldliness, transcendence of ordinary humanness	Eternal Self-Subsistence (*ṣamadāniyya*)	Satan (*shayṭān*)
VIGILANCE (*sahar*)	Cultivating the moment	Cultivating the moment, assuming lordly attributes	Everlasting Self-Existence (*qayyūmiyya*)	The self (*nafs*)

if they have real validity, and every spiritual tradition knows of their efficacy.

Finally, it is worth noting that the number four plays a significant role in Ibn ʿArabī's thought. Elsewhere he refers to it as the most perfect number,[43] and associates it with the earthly, receptive principle (as opposed to the heavenly, active principle): for example, the four sub-lunar spheres, the four qualities of Universal Nature or the four categories of existence. In the *Ḥilyat al-abdāl* the four pillars or exterior principles are the prerequisites for spiritual ascension. The pillars correspond, then, in a certain sense, to the *isrā*, the overland nocturnal journey from Mecca to Jerusalem accomplished by the Prophet prior to his ascension into heaven (*miʿrāj*), an Abrahamic spiritual journey from the "place of Ishmael" to the "place of Isaac", a purification process that takes the seeker to a place beyond the four exterior dimensions. Only through the accomplishment of these four, says Ibn ʿArabī, will the reality of the *abdāl* be known, the seven representatives of Heaven who are described in the final poem as "those of pure virtue and noble eminence".

43. See *Tarjumān al-ashwāq*, p.124 (in the commentary to poem XL).

THE ADORNMENT OF THE SPIRITUALLY TRANSFORMED (*ḤILYAT AL-ABDĀL*)

TRANSLATION

In the Name of God, the All-Compassionate, the Most Merciful, and may the blessings of God be upon our master Muhammad and all his family

THE ADORNMENT OF THE SPIRITUALLY TRANSFORMED

AND THOSE SPIRITUAL KNOWLEDGES AND STATES THAT MANIFEST FROM IT

Our master and leader, the shaykh, the imām, the gnostic, the verifier, the best of the Prophet's own circle (*al-salaf*)[1] and the support of those who follow (*al-khalaf*), Muḥyī al-dīn Abū ʿAbd Allāh Muḥammad b. ʿAlī ibn Muḥammad Ibn al-ʿArabī al-Ṭā'ī al-Ḥātimī al-Andalusī, may God be pleased with him, says:

Praise be to God for what He has granted as inspiration and for making known to us that which we did not know. God's grace towards us has been tremendous.[2] May God's blessings be upon our most honourable master, who was granted the totality of the Words[3] in the supreme abode, and may He greet him with salutations of peace.

1. Ar: *baqiyyat al-salaf.* This could also be translated as 'the remaining portion of the Prophet's own circle'.

2. Cf. Q.4.113: "God has sent down upon you the Book and Wisdom, and has made known to you that which you did not know. God's grace towards you has been tremendous."

3. Ar: *jawāmiʿ al-kalim* (mentioned in several *ḥadīths*, e.g. Ibn Hanbal, *Musnad* II. 411–12, and Muslim, *Masājid*, 5–8). One could translate this also as "the ability to reunite the Words", alluding to the completion of the prophetic revelation in Muhammad. This capacity is mentioned as one of the six defining characteristics of the "Seal of the Prophets", which no previous prophet had received: "I have been granted the totality of the Words; I have been rescued by terror (cast into the hearts of my enemies); booty has been made legal for me; the whole earth has been established for me as a place of prayer and a means of purification; I have been sent to all creatures, and through me the prophets are sealed."

I consulted God on Sunday night the 12th of Jumāda II in the year 599,[4] at the place of Āl Mayyah in Ṭā'if,[5] during a visit to [the tomb of] 'Abd Allāh Ibn 'Abbās, the Prophet's cousin.[6] This was because of a request by my companions Abū Muḥammad 'Abd Allāh Badr b. 'Abd Allāh al-Ḥabashī,[7] the freed slave of Abū al-Ghanā'im b. Abī al-Futūḥ al-Ḥarrānī (may God have mercy on him), and Abū 'Abd Allāh Muḥammad b. Khālid al-Ṣadafī al-Tilimsānī,[8] may God grant them both success! They asked me to write for them, during the time of this visit, something from which they could benefit concerning the Path of the hereafter (*ṭarīq al-ākhira*). So I made my appeal to God for this, and wrote for them this short treatise which I have entitled: "The Adornment of the Spiritually Transformed and those spiritual knowledges and states which manifest from it", that it may be of assistance for them and others upon the Path to true happiness, and a chapter that brings together the various forms of spiritual

4. 27 January 1203.

5. Tā'if is a walled city two days' journey south of Mecca, known as the "garden of the Hijaz" because of its good climate and green fields. In his *Fihrist* Ibn 'Arabī specifies that he was staying in the road of Āl Mayyah, but it is unclear what this name refers to. It is not to be confused with the beloved of Ghaylān (Mayya), nor with the subdivision al-Mayyāḥ of the Rabī'a tribe, who lived west of the Tigris.

6. Ibn 'Abbās, who died in Tā'if in AH 68 (AD 687), was the son of the Prophet's uncle and great-grandson of Hāshim, from whom the Banū Hāshim take their ancestry. Known as one of the most important early authorities on *fiqh* (jurisprudence), *ḥadīth* (stories of the Prophet's sayings and actions) and *tafsīr* (interpretation of the Quran), Ibn 'Abbās was also a progenitor of the 'Abbāsid caliphate, which supplanted the Umayyads. Ibn 'Arabī refers to Ibn 'Abbās as one of the singulars (*afrād*), and elsewhere quotes his saying: "If I were to explain the true meaning (of a particular Quranic verse), you would stone me for being an unbeliever."

7. Al-Ḥabashī was the close companion of Ibn 'Arabī for some 24 years, from around the time of the Shaykh's ascension in Fez in 594/1197 until he died in Malatya in 618/1221, a faithful servant and transmitter of the master's oral teachings. He related several *ḥadīth*s to Ibn 'Arabī, which were written down in the *Mishkāt al-Anwār* (see Hirtenstein and Notcutt, *Divine Sayings*, p. 109). See also his *K. al-Inbāh*, translated by Denis Gril.

8. A close companion of Ibn 'Arabī during his stay in Mecca, Muḥammad b. Khālid al-Ṣadafī acted as transmitter to Ibn 'Arabī for seven of the *ḥadīth*s collected in the *Mishkāt al-Anwār* (see Hirtenstein and Notcutt, *Divine Sayings*, p. 109).

desire (*irāda*).[9] From the One who has bestowed existence upon the world we beg support and help!

True Governance (*ḥukm*) is the fruit of Wisdom (*ḥikma*), and True Knowledge (*ʿilm*) is the fruit of Gnosis (*maʿrifa*).[10] Thus one who does not possess wisdom has no true governance, while one who does not possess gnosis has no true knowledge. The one who possesses true governance and knowledge (*al-ḥākim al-ʿālim*) belongs [utterly] to God, firmly existent (*lillāh qāʾim*), whereas the one who possesses wisdom and gnosis (*al-ḥakīm al-ʿārif*) exists through God, halted (*billāh wāqif*).[11] Those with true governance and knowledge are the people of the [letter] *Lām*, and those with wisdom and gnosis are the people of the [letter] *Bāʾ*.[12]

9. *Irāda* can be translated as both will and desire: when applied to the Divine, it signifies the Divine Will which bestows being, i.e. that God says 'Be' to each thing. However, here the emphasis is on the different kinds of spiritual aspiration or desire on the part of the human: the renunciate (*zāhid*), the one who trusts in God (*mutawakkil*), the aspirant (*murīd*), the worshipper (*ʿābid*), and the gnostic (*ʿārif*).

10. According to Ibn ʿArabī, the principle of real rulership or governance, which involves the exercise of authority, is a higher stage than wisdom (both from the same Arabic root, *ḥ-k-m*), since it involves the fullest expression in action of the Divine Name the Wise, as exemplified in the kingship of Solomon. Likewise, Knowledge derives from the Divine Name the Knower (*ʿalīm*), which is a higher degree than experiential gnosis (*maʿrifa*); this can be compared to the distinction between coming to know something and knowing it fully in the manner that God knows. As Ibn ʿArabī explains in his *Iṣṭilāhāt al-ṣūfiyya*, the *ʿārif* is overwhelmed by spiritual states while the *ʿālim* (one who fully actualizes Knowledge) is not.

11. These two degrees are referred to more explicitly elsewhere by Ibn ʿArabī: the true knowers who "return" from union with God in order to direct and guide others, and the gnostics who return in order to perfect themselves (see Chodkiewicz, *Seal of the Saints*, pp. 170ff.). The first group is considered higher due to their completion of the Station of Inheritance: they have realized the full meaning of union, i.e. that His Essence is the Existent and there is no other.

12. The difference between the letters *Lām* and *Bāʾ* can be explained with reference to the first two words of the *Sūrat al-Fātiḥa*: *al-ḥamdu lillāh* (Praise belongs to God). Following Ibn ʿArabī, the famous Algerian leader and mystic Emir ʿAbd al-

The renunciate zealously abandons his life in this world, and the one who trusts in God passionately entrusts his affairs to his Master; and the aspirant is taken up with audition and ecstatic states, and the worshipper fervently renders worship and strives in devotion; and the person of wisdom and gnosis is enamoured of his spiritual will and resolve. Yet those who possess true knowledge and spiritual governance are concealed in the World of the Unseen (*ghayb*), so that they are unknown to the gnostic, aspirant or worshipper, and they are invisible to the one who trusts in God and the one who renounces the world. For the renunciate abandons [the world] for the purpose of being recompensed; the entruster fides [in God] to attain the object of his desire; the aspirant seeks ecstasy to relieve distress; the worshipper strives hard in his longing for closeness; and the wise gnostic through his spiritual will aims at union. However, the Real God (*ḥaqq*) only reveals Himself to one who can no longer be described or named at all.

Gnosis is a veil over the One cognosed, and wisdom a door before which one halts. What remains that can be described are causes, like the letters, and these are all secondary effects (*ʿilal*),[13] blinding vision and blotting out light. If the created world (*kawn*) did not exist, the Essence (*ʿayn*) would have manifested; if there were no Names, the

---

Qādir al-Jazā'iri distinguished three kinds of people: the ordinary believers who praise God through themselves (*bi-anfusihim*); the elite who praise God through God (*bi-llāh*), and the elite of the elite whose praise of God belongs to God (*li-llāh*). The second group, who are the people of *Bā'* (from *bi Allāh*), know that they render praise through God's being their tongue: their existence is clothed in the Divine attributes. They are inferior to the third group, the people of *Lām* (from *li Allāh*), who know that it is God Himself who renders His Own praise through their tongue: the Divine Existence is clothed in their attributes. These two aspects of sainthood are also referred to respectively as the closeness of supererogation (*nawāfil*) and the closeness of obligation (*farā'iḍ*).

13. Ibn ʿArabī is playing here with the triple meaning of the word *ʿilal*, which means (a) an effect of a cause; (b) weakness, excuse or pretext; and (c) cause or reason. By contrasting it with the word *sabab* (cause), Ibn ʿArabī intends to explain that what we take as a [secondary] cause is also an effect, or even a defect, as God is the One who causes all things, be they apparently effects or causes.

Named would have appeared; were there no original love, then the union would have endured; were there no apportioning, the degrees would have been overruled. If there were no He-ness (*huwiyya*), the I-ness (*aniyya*) would have manifested; if there were no He, then He would have become existent; if there were no You, then the mark of ignorance would have been totally obvious. If there were no [veiled] understanding, then true knowledge would have established its supremacy. Then would these dark clouds of oppression have dispersed, and this army of doubt (*buham*)[14] would have been dispatched by the sharp swords of annihilation!

He who dwells therein forever, in the mysteries of Eternity,
revealed Himself to your heart.
But what veils the Essence from Its own attainment is none
other than you, though this be merely speaking in imagery.
It became clear to the heart that the One whom it saw has
dwelt therein always and forever;
thereupon came a Divine Address, replete with words, its
radiance manifesting the contours of the place.

At Marchena of the Olives in al-Andalus[15] we once had a companion, one of the men of sanctity (*al-sālihīn*), who used to teach the Quran. He was an excellent jurist, who knew the Quran and hadith by heart, a man of piety and merit who served the poor (*fuqarā'*). His name

14. This is a complex image which suggests several interrelated meanings: *buham* (as vowelled in Y, rhyming here with *ẓulam*) is the plural of *buhma*, signifying a mass of hard stone or an army which appears unbeatable, as well as confused or dubious affairs. In addition, it refers to the three nights in which the moon does not visibly rise, a darkness that is only dispelled by the appearance of the new moon. The root's other meanings are also implied: vagueness and confusion (*ibhām*), that which is locked up and shut (for example, a heart which is impenetrable to admonition, *mubham*), young lambs or goats (*baham*) and brutishness (*bahīma*).

15. The small town of Marchena is situated some 45 km south-east of Seville in modern Andalusia, but little remains of its Arab past.

was ʿAbd al-Majīd b. Salama. He, may God grant him success, once told me of the following incident:

> One night I was praying, and I had just finished my prayer (*ḥizb*) and had put my head between my knees invoking God when I felt someone's presence. This person pulled out my prayer-mat from under me and replaced it with a palm-leaf mat. Then he said to me: "Perform your prayers on that!" Now the door to my house was shut and fear of him took hold of me. He said to me: "One who enjoys intimacy with God feels no fear."[16] Then he added: "But fear God in every state." Then I had an inspiration and asked him: "O my lord, by what means do the Substitutes become Substitutes?", to which he replied: "By the four things which Abū Ṭālib [al-Makkī] mentioned in the Qūt [al-Qulūb]: silence, seclusion, hunger and vigilance." Then he left me, without my having a clue as to how he had come in or how he had gone out, for my door remained closed and the palm-leaf mat was still under me.

This man was one of the Substitutes, whose name was Muʿādh Ibn Ashras, may God be satisfied with him.[17] The four things which he mentioned are the supports of this most radiant Way and its foundations. One who does not involve himself in them or is not deeply grounded in them strays from the Way of God, exalted is He! Our objective in these pages is to speak of these things in four separate sections, and discuss what they bestow of spiritual knowledges and states. May God make us and you of those who are realized in them and permanently established in them! Indeed He has full ability and power to do that.

16. K adds "of other than Him".

17. See the slightly different version given in Appendix A, p. 43, which also appears in Ibn ʿArabī's *Rūḥ al-quds* – see Austin, *Sufis of Andalusia*, p. 151 (from *Durrat al-fākhira*).

Silence (ṣamt)

There are two kinds of silence: firstly, silence of the tongue, which consists of not speaking of other than God the Exalted with other than God the Exalted, altogether; and secondly, silence of the heart, which consists of refraining from all thought occurring in the soul that concerns any created thing at all. The one whose tongue is silent, even if his heart is not, lightens his burden. When someone's tongue and heart are both silent, his inmost consciousness (*sirr*) is manifest and his Lord reveals Himself to him. The one whose heart is silent but whose tongue is not is a speaker with the tongue of wisdom. The one who does not possess either a silent tongue or a silent heart is under the domination of Satan and an object of his ridicule.

The silence of the tongue is one of the abodes of everyone and of all seekers (*sālikūn*). The silence of the heart is one of the [distinctive] qualities of those brought close (*muqarrabūn*), who are people of true contemplation. The state that silence brings the seekers is safety from all harm, while the state that it brings those brought close is intimate converse [with God]. He who maintains silence in all states has no speech except with his Lord. Complete silence of the tongue within is impossible for the human being: thus if he withdraws from talking with others in favour of converse with his Lord, he becomes delivered, brought close, one who is endorsed in his speech when he speaks, and does so according to what is proper and hits the mark, for he speaks "out of God" (*ʿan Allāh*), exalted is He. God has said with regard to His Prophet: "And he does not speak out of passion." Speaking according to what is proper is the fruit of silence, which is refraining from error. Conversing with other than God is an error in every case, and speaking of other than God is bad in every respect.

God says: "There is no good in much of their secret discourse, except for one who enjoins alms-giving or what is equitable or promotes reconciliation amongst people",[18] observing all their conditions. God

18. Q.4.114.

also says: "They were given no order except to worship God, pure in devotion to Him."[19]

Connected to the state of silence is the station of Inspiration (*wahy*), in its various forms.

Silence bequeaths knowledge of God (Allāh), exalted is He.

Seclusion ('uzla)[20]

Seclusion leads to silence for man, since one who withdraws from human company has no-one to talk to, and that naturally leads to silence of the tongue. There are two kinds of seclusion: firstly, the seclusion of the aspirants (*murīdūn*), which consists of not associating physically with others; and secondly, the seclusion of the verifiers (*muhaqqiqūn*), which consists of having no contact with created things in one's heart: their hearts have no room for anything other than the knowledge of God, exalted is He, which is the witness of the Truth in the heart that results from contemplation.[21]

The people of seclusion have three motives: (a) the fear of the evil of other people affecting oneself; (b) the fear of one's own evil affecting others – this is a higher [perception] than the first, as in the first case one thinks badly of others, while in the second one thinks badly of oneself, and thinking badly of oneself is better since you are more knowledgeable of yourself; (c) the preference for the company of the Master from the Sublime Assembly – the most elevated of men is one who parts from himself out of preference for the company of his

19. Q.98.5.

20. The root *'-z-l* means to put something aside or separate, and in the eighth form has the connotations of separating oneself or withdrawing from association with others (hence the theologians known as the Mu'tazila who seceded from other groups). *'Uzla* for Ibn 'Arabī denotes a seclusion or separation which may be external or internal.

21. The "witness" (*shāhid*) is defined by Ibn 'Arabī as "that which remains in the servant's heart after he has separated from the station of contemplation (*mushāhada*, from the same root as *shāhid*)" (*K. al-Shawāhid*, p. 1) and "what the heart retains of the form of the One contemplated" (*Iṣṭilāhāt*).

Lord. One who prefers seclusion to the company of others prefers his Lord to that which is other than Him. And no-one can know what gifts and mysteries God showers upon the one who prefers his Lord. Seclusion never happens in the heart unless the heart feels an estrangement from that which one is separating from, and an intimacy with the One with whom one is secluding oneself, which is what drives one into seclusion.

Seclusion has no need of the [extra] condition of silence, as silence is necessarily included within it, insofar as it is silence of the tongue. As for silence of the heart, seclusion does not necessarily lead to it, since one could converse with oneself about other than God and with other than God, exalted is He. This is why we have considered silence to be one of the pillars (*arkān*) on the Way in its own right.

One who makes seclusion their practice grasps the mystery of the Divine Unity (*wahdāniyya*). In terms of knowledges and mysteries, this brings to him the secrets of the Uniqueness (*aḥadiyya)* insofar as it is a quality. The true spiritual state of seclusion, whether it be that of the seeker or the verifier, is to be transcendent of all attributes. The highest state of seclusion is retreat (*khalwa*), for it is a seclusion within seclusion, and its fruit is stronger than that of ordinary seclusion. One who makes seclusion his practice must have certainty regarding God, exalted is He, until he has no thought that will distract him and take him beyond the confines of his seclusion. If he lacks certainty, then let him prepare himself to be strong enough for seclusion, in order that his certainty may be strengthened by what is revealed to him in his seclusion. There is no other way. This is one of the firm preconditions governing seclusion.

Seclusion bequeaths knowledge of this world (*dunyā*).

Hunger (*jūʿ*)[22]

Hunger is the third pillar of this Divine Way. It includes the fourth pillar, which is vigilance, in the same way that seclusion includes silence. There are two kinds of hunger: voluntary hunger, which is that of the seekers, and obligatory (involuntary) hunger, which is that of the verifiers. The verifier does not impose hunger on himself: rather, his physical nourishment decreases when he is in the station of intimacy (*uns*), and increases when he is the station of awe (*hayba*). When the verifiers eat a large quantity of food, it is a sure sign of the force with which the lights of Reality rush upon their hearts in their contemplation of Majestic Grandeur (*ʿaẓama*). Eating a small amount of food, on the other hand, is a sure sign of the converse they enjoy in their contemplation of Intimacy. For the seekers, an increase in food indicates their distance from God, exalted is He, their banishment from His Door, and their enslavement to the covetous animal self through its domination of them. For them a decrease in food indicates that scents of Divine Generosity are passing over their hearts, causing them to be oblivious to their bodily needs.

Hunger is, in every state and every respect, a means whereby the seeker and the verifier can attain to a more exalted degree, for the seeker in terms of spiritual states, for the verifier in terms of mysteries. One who practises hunger should not overdo the period of being in a state of alertness, since an excess in this respect leads to delusion and loss of reason, as well as a weakening of physical health. There is no way that a seeker should practise hunger in order to attain spiritual states except under the direction of a spiritual master; if he has none, it is still not possible, although in this case he may reduce the quantity of food he eats and observe ordinary fasting and eating only one meal a day. Should he want to eat a fatty stew with meat, let him

22. Ibn ʿArabī is careful to distinguish this "emptiness of the belly" from the particular practice of fasting (*ṣawm*). The root also suggests desire and longing, as in "being hungry for something".

not do so more than twice a week if he wants to have benefit, until he finds a master. When he has found one, he should place himself in his hands, and the master will look after him and his affairs, since he knows better than he does what is most beneficial for him.

Hunger has a spiritual state and a station. It is characterized by humility, submission, servility, lack of self-importance, indigence, discretion, tranquil emotions and an absence of base thoughts – this is the state the seeker has. For the verifiers its state consists of delicacy of feeling, serenity, intimacy [with God], disappearance of worldliness and transcendence of ordinary human characteristics through the Divine Might and Lordly Dominion. As a station, it is the station of Eternal Self-Subsistence (*al-maqām al-ṣamadānī*), a most elevated station characterized by mysteries, revelations and states. We have already mentioned this in our book *Mawāqiʿ an-Nujūm*, in the section on the organ of the Heart.[23] However, it is only in certain copies of the book, as I finished writing this point in the town of Bijāya in the year 597,[24] after several copies that did not contain details of this spiritual abode (*manzil*) had already come out.

This, then, is the benefit of hunger for the one who possesses spiritual intention (*himma*), not ordinary hunger. For ordinary [physical] hunger restores good temperament and brings bodily health, nothing more.

Hunger bequeaths knowledge of Satan, may God preserve us and you from him.

23. See *Mawāqiʿ an-Nujūm*, p. 145. The piece referred to is part of a long section devoted to the sphere of the Heart and is entitled "the Abode of Revelation of the Self-Subsistent, the Odd".

24. Bijāya (Bougie) is a coastal town in modern Algeria, where the great Maghribi master Abū Madyan lived and taught for many years. After visiting Abū Madyan's tomb near Tlemcen, Ibn ʿArabī stayed in the town in Ramaḍān 597 (June 1201), during his journey from Marrakesh to Tunis when he left the Maghrib for good.

Vigilance (sahar)[25]

Vigilance is the fruit of hunger, for an empty stomach drives away sleep. There are two kinds of vigilance: vigil of the eye and vigil of the heart. The heart's vigil is awakening from the sleep of forgetfulness and seeking contemplation, while the eye's vigil is the desire to maintain the spiritual intention in the heart to pursue the quest for night-converse (*musāmara*). For when the eye sleeps, the activity of the heart ceases, but if the heart is not asleep when the eye is, its objective is contemplation of its previous vigil, no more. Indeed, for the heart to observe anything else is not possible. The benefit of vigil is in keeping the heart active and in ascending to the high abodes which lie in the safekeeping of God, exalted is He.

The spiritual state of vigilance is to cultivate the present moment, for both the seeker and the verifier, except that the verifier also has an increase in assuming the lordly attributes (*takhalluq rabbānī*), unknown to the seeker. Its spiritual station is that of Everlasting Self-Existence (*qayyūmīya*). Sometimes some of our companions have declared it impossible that someone could be realized (*taḥaqquq*) in Self-Existence, while others could not admit the possibility of assuming its attributes (*takhalluq*).[26] I myself met ʿAbd Allāh b. Junayd[27] and found that he denied this possibility. As for us, we do not agree

25. The word *sahar* specifically means being awake at night, abstaining from sleep, and this is why Ibn ʿArabī describes it as an action of refraining. It is not only keeping vigil while others sleep, but also the condition of wakefulness or vigilance. It is equally used to describe a camel that gives milk abundantly (*sāhirat al-ʿirq*) and a spring or fountain that runs night and day (*sāhirat al-ʿayn*) (see Lane's *Lexicon*, 4, s-h-r). This meaning of continuity and constancy is clearly linked to the notion of *qayyūmīya*, which Ibn ʿArabī mentions below.

26. *Takhalluq* and its complements (*taḥaqquq*, *taʿalluq*) are important technical terms in Ibn ʿArabī's terminology. In his *Kashf al-maʿnā*, he describes each Divine Name under these three interrelated headings: *taʿalluq* denotes the way the Name is related to the Essence; *taḥaqquq* the realization of the qualities of the Name as they relate to the Divine and to the servant; *takhalluq* the way in which the servant is manifested with these qualities. See Arabic edition and Spanish translation by Pablo Beneito, *El Secreto de los Nombres de Dios*.

with that view, since the realities have shown us that for the Perfect Man there exists no Name in the Divine Presence that he is not the bearer of. If there is anyone of our company who is undecided about this question, that is due to his lack of true knowledge concerning what Man is in his essential reality and origin. If he knew himself, this matter would not be difficult for him.

Vigilance bequeaths knowledge of the self.

The pillars (*arkān*) of spiritual knowledge are complete when knowledge revolves around the acquisition of these four: knowledge of God, of the self, of this world and of Satan. When man withdraws from the created world and from himself, and when he silences his own internal voice, leaving space for his Lord's mentioning of him, and when he relinquishes corporeal nourishment and remains wakeful while others are plunged in sleep: when these four properties have been united in him, then his humanity is transmuted[28] into angelic nature and his servanthood into mastery; his intellect (*'aql*) becomes a sense faculty, his invisible reality (*ghayb*) becomes visible, and his interior becomes manifest.

27. Ibn 'Arabī states that he met this man, whom he calls a shaykh (i.e. a spiritual master) and a Mu'tazilī (i.e. an adherent of an important theological movement that stressed the absolute transcendence of God), at his place in Qabrafīq near Ronda. Apparently they discussed the question of whether men could assume the attribute of the Divine Name *al-Qayyūm*, and Ibn 'Arabī persuaded him and his students to his way of thinking, based on the Quranic verse that states that "men are superior (*qawwām*) to women" (Q.4.34). See *Fut.*II.182, III.45 and IV.79.

28. Here Ibn 'Arabī uses the root *b-d-l*, the same as that of Substitutes (*abdāl*), in the sense of "exchanging" one set of qualifications for another, suggesting that the *abdāl* are those who have undergone a total transformation, and their earthly qualities have been transmuted into heavenly ones. It is a permanent change, echoed in the Quranic verses: "on the Day when the earth shall be changed into another earth, and the heavens likewise" (Q.14.48) and "God shall change their evil deeds into good deeds" (Q.25.70).

Then if he leaves the place where he is, he leaves behind his "substitute" (*badal*), a spiritual reality which can be encountered by the spirits of the people of the place this saint has left. If a resident of that place conceives a strong desire to see this person, then that spiritual reality which he left behind as his substitute will take on sensible form for them. He talks to them and they talk to him. They imagine that he really is the one they are talking to, when in fact he is not there, until he has finished what he needed to do. This spiritual being can also take on bodily form when its owner himself conceives a strong desire for or connects his spiritual will to that place. This can even happen to someone other than a Substitute. The difference between these two situations is that when the true Substitute leaves, he knows that he has left behind his "substitute", while he who is not a Substitute is not aware of that, even though he has actually left one behind. This is because the latter is not master of these four pillars that we have mentioned.

And regarding this I[29] say:

> O you who desire the spiritual abodes of the Substitutes,
> without aspiring to the requisite actions,
> Do not hanker after them in vain, for you cannot be one of
> them without emulating their spiritual states.
> Silence your heart, seclude yourself from all that brings you
> down to other than the Beloved Master,
> Be wakeful and hunger. Thus shall you be given their station
> and their company, in all your coming and going.
> The House of Sainthood has various pillars, and our
> masters who live there are of the Substitutes.
> Amidst silence and seclusion unceasing, hunger and
> vigilance, live those of pure virtue and noble eminence!

May God grant us and you success in accomplishing these pillars, and may He accord us the grace of the abodes of perfection (*ihsān*). Indeed He is the most Munificent Friend!

29. That is, in the following poem Ibn 'Arabī is speaking with his own voice, as one person to another, rather than as the inspired author of the treatise.

APPENDIX A

The Nine Principles of Goodness

A Translation of Chapter 53 of *al-Futūḥāt al-Makkīya*[1]

If you haven't encountered a teacher, then be as someone who
takes refuge,
who disciplines his soul, and breaks up the night into portions[2]
for glorifying and reciting (*qur'ān*), made sleepless by the One
who faces him,[3]
the One who smites him down and revives him. When he stops
asking "what on earth...?",
then he attains his desire, [becoming] a student and [finding]
a Teacher.
Knowledge of Him comes to him, in groups and alone.
This I have elucidated for him, so that he may not be cut off
from it.

Know – may God aid you and grant you light! – that the first thing that is incumbent upon one who has just joined this Path of Divine

1. *Fut*.I.277–8. The full title of the chapter is "regarding the knowledge of what actions the seeker may impose upon himself prior to finding the Master". Bearing in mind that there is nothing but Him in existence, then God is the True Master, and the image of the human teacher is nothing but a means of bringing down His teaching.

2. Ar: *aflādhan*, which means pieces or slices (e.g. of meat), i.e. that the night is broken up into pieces by the person arising in prayer. The word is also used in the expression *aflādh al-arḍ*, meaning the hidden treasures of the earth, and it may be that Ibn ʿArabī also has this connotation in mind.

3. This could also be translated as "the One who confronts him", standing in front of him as on the battle-field. The Divine is here portrayed as the Lover who brooks no resistance. This meaning fits well with the next line, which reads *aṣʿaqahu* (smote him) in the original manuscript instead of *aḍʿafahu* (weakened him) in the printed Beirut edition.

prescription is that he should seek the teacher (*ustādh*) until he finds him. During the time while he is searching for the teacher, let him undertake the actions which I shall enumerate below.

There are nine things which he should impose upon himself, and these are the very principles of number. When he acts upon them, he becomes firmly established in affirmation of Unity (*tawḥīd*). For this reason God caused there to be nine celestial spheres.[4] So contemplate what appears of Divine Wisdom in the orbits of these nine. There are four of them in your exterior, five in your interior.

Those in your exterior are: hunger (*jūʿ*), vigilance (*sahar*), silence (*ṣamt*) and seclusion (*ʿuzla*). The two active ones are hunger and seclusion, while the two receptive ones are vigilance and silence. I mean by silence abstaining from speaking with people, and being occupied with the remembrance of the heart and the real expression of the self[5] rather than the speaking of the tongue, except when God commands it, such as the recitation of the *Fātiḥa*[6] or the part of the Quran which is recited in the ritual prayer, and the magnificat (*takbīr*) therein, and whatever is prescribed of glorification, remembrance, supplication, bearing witness to Him[7] and blessing the Envoy of God, peace and blessings be upon him, until you are thereby in submission. Then you are free to devote yourself to the remembrance of the heart with the silence of the tongue. Hunger includes vigilance, and solitude includes silence.

As for the five interior ones, they are: veracity (*sidq*), trust (*tawakkul*), patience (*ṣabr*), resolution (*ʿazīma*) and certainty (*yaqīn*).

These nine are the mothers of all good, and they include all

4. These nine are the Moon, Mercury, Venus, Sun, Mars, Jupiter, Saturn, the fixed stars and the starless sphere. See Chittick, *The Self-Disclosure of God*, pp. xxx–xxxi.

5. Ar: *nuṭq al-nafs*, referring to *al-nafs al-nāṭiqa*, the "speaking soul" which is the true human reality of the self, as opposed to *al-nafs al-ḥayawāniya*, the "animal/bestial soul".

6. Literally, the Mother of the Quran (*umm al-qur'ān*).

7. Ar: *tashahhud*, bearing witness to the Divine means here saying "there is no god but God".

that is good. The whole Path is included in them. So practise them constantly until you find the Master.

Let me now mention to you something of the nature of each one of these qualities which will incite you to act upon them and persevere in them. May God cause us and you to profit and be of the people of His Providential Care!

We shall begin with the exterior ones first and say:

Seclusion is the chief of the four considerations which we have mentioned, according to the People of God (*ṭā'ifa*). I was informed (of this) by my brother in God, ʿAbd al-Majīd b. Salama, preacher at Marchena of the Olives, in the province of Seville in al-Andalus, and he was one of those who strove assiduously in worship. He told me the following story in AH 586:

> I was in my house in Marchena one evening, doing my night-prayers (*hizb*). I was in the middle of my prayer, with the door of the house and the door of the room fastened, when suddenly a man appeared and greeted me. I had no idea how he had got in. I was extremely worried about him and quickly completed my prayer. When I greeted him, he said to me: "O ʿAbd al-Majīd! One who enjoys intimacy with God feels no fear." Then he took up the cloth which was under me as a prayer-mat, and threw it away. He unrolled a small straw-mat that he had with him and said to me: "Now do your prayers upon this!" He then took me outside the house and then out of the country, and walked with me in a land I did not know. I had no idea at all where on God's earth I was, but God the Exalted has informed us of these places. Then he returned me to my home where I lived. Then I asked him: "O my brother! By what means do the *abdāl* become *abdāl*?" and he replied: "Through the four things that Abū Ṭālib [al-Makkī] mentioned in the Qūt [al-Qulūb]", namely hunger, vigilance, silence and seclusion.

Then ʿAbd al-Majīd showed me the mat, and I did my prayer on it. This man was one of the greatest of them, and was called Muʿādh Ibn Ashras.

Seclusion

Seclusion occurs when the seeker withdraws himself from every negative quality and every low characteristic. That is being secluded in his (interior) state. As for seclusion in his heart, that is when he withdraws himself in his heart from attachment to any one of God's creatures, be it family, possessions, children, friends or anything that intervenes between him and the remembrance of his Lord in his heart, or even the thought of it. Rather, he has but one interest and concern: his attachment to God.

On the external level, being secluded consists, at the beginning of one's spiritual journey, of separating oneself from people and all that is familiar, whether at home or abroad on God's earth. If one is in a town, it should be somewhere one is not known; if not in a town, then it should be at the coast or in the mountains so long as one is far from people. If wild animals become friendly and familiar with one and God causes them to speak, whether in words or not, then one should seclude oneself from wild beasts and animals, and request of God the Exalted that one is not occupied with other than Him, and persevere in the hidden remembrance (*dhikr al-khafī*).[8] If one is a person who knows the Quran by heart, one should take a part of it for recital every night, remaining with it in prayer so that one does not forget it. There should not be a lot of specific prayers or moving about. One should always come back to being occupied with Him in one's heart. This should become one's constant habit and practice.

8. This is one's personal *dhikr*, as opposed to *dhikr al-awqāt* which is done at the end of ritual prayer as supererogatory or *dhikr al-ḥaḍra* which is done communally.

Silence

Silence consists of not speaking to any created thing, wild beast or insect, that accompanies one while one is travelling or in the places of one's seclusion. If any of the jinn or the highest assembly[9] appear, one should close one's eyes to them and not engage in conversation with them, even if they speak. If an answer is required, one should give it exactly as required, and no more. If an answer is not needed, one should keep silent and be occupied with one's own work. When they see the person in this state, they will keep away from him and not get in his way and hide themselves from him. For they know that whoever distracts someone who is busy with God from his occupation with Him is punished by God most severely.

As for being silent in oneself from the chatter of the self, one should not talk to oneself about what one hopes to obtain from God, as regards what is allotted to one. That is a waste of time without any gain, as it is just a desire. If one gets used to the chatter of the self, it prevents the remembrance of God in the heart, because the heart cannot include both chatter and remembrance together. Then one misses out on the very reason for going into seclusion and silence, which is the remembrance of God the Most High by which the mirror of his heart is polished.[10] For this is how one's Lord is revealed.

9. Ar: *al-malā' al-a'lā*, signifying the angels and spiritual beings that inhabit the higher world. Sometimes they are contrasted with *al-malā' al-adnā* or *al-asfal*, the creatures of the corporeal world.

10. Ibn 'Arabī is here playing with the two meanings of the root *j-l-y*: to polish and clean, and to reveal or make manifest. When the heart is polished, then it can truly reflect the Divine revelation.

Hunger

Hunger is reduction in food. One should not partake of it except in order to stand upright in worship of one's Lord, in the obligatory prayers. As for supererogatory prayer, sitting down when one is too weak due to lack of nourishment is better, more preferable and stronger in attaining what is desired from God than having the strength that comes from food in order to perform the supererogatory prayers standing up. Fullness leads to excess. When the belly is full, then the limbs dominate and act with excess, be it in terms of movement, looking, listening or conversation. All of this takes one away from the aim and intention.

Vigilance

This is the result of hunger because of a lack of humidity and the vapours that cause sleep, especially the drinking of water, for that causes sleep and the desire for it is a delusion. The real benefit of vigilance lies in rousing oneself for the sake of being occupied with God in whatever one is busy with, constantly. When one sleeps, one is transported to the intermediate world (*barzakh*) in accordance with what one went to sleep with, nothing more. Great good eludes one, which one does not know except in the state of wakefulness. If one perseveres in this, vigilance pervades the eye of the heart (*'ayn al-qalb*), and the eye of inner vision (*'ayn al-basīra*) is unveiled through adhering to remembrance. Then one sees whatever good God the Exalted wishes.

In the practice of these lie four things which are the foundation of knowledge for the people of God, to which Ḥārith b. Asad al-Muḥāsibī[11] devoted himself more than anyone else. They are: knowledge of God (*Allāh*), knowledge of the soul (*nafs*), knowledge of this world (*dunyā*) and knowledge of Satan. Some people have mentioned knowledge of passion (*hawā*) instead of knowledge of God, quoting the following [verses]:

> I am afflicted by those four [enemies] that have pelted me
> with arrows, from a bow tightly drawn:
> Iblīs, the world, my soul and passion –
> O Lord, You [alone] are able to deliver [me]!

And as another has said:

> Iblīs, the world, my soul and passion –
> how can there be deliverance while they all assail me?

As for the five interior things, they were related to me by my righteous wife, Maryam bt. Muḥammad b. ʿAbdūn b. ʿAbd al-Raḥmān al-Bijāʾī.[12] She said: "I have seen in my dream a person who often visits me in my visions (*waqāʿī*) but who I have never met in the flesh." He

11. One of the great figures of early Islam (AH 165–243 / AD 781–857), who emphasized examining (*hasab*) the self, and imposed extreme discipline upon himself. Many Sufis were sceptical of his approach since they felt it tended to make one judge one's own action, a role which is best left to God. Born in Basra, he spent the greater part of his life in Baghdad, where he had many students, including Junayd. He wrote several books, including *K. Muḥāsabat al-nufūs* (The Book of Examining the Selves), in which he described these four knowledges, and which evidently influenced Ibn ʿArabī's own *Rūḥ al-Quds fī muḥāsabat an-nafs*. He wrote: "For 30 years my ear listened to nothing but my own conscience, but for 30 years since then my state has been such that my conscience has listened to none but God." See Austin, *Sufis of Andalusia*, pp. 87 and 115; also Margaret Smith, *An Early Mystic of Baghdad: a Study of the Life and Teaching of Ḥārith b. Asad al-Muḥāsibī*.

12. Maryam was almost certainly Ibn ʿArabī's second wife, who is referred to by his stepson, Ṣadruddīn al-Qūnawī, as "Khātūn Maryam bint ʿAbd Allāh, mother of ʿAlāʾuddīn Muḥammad, known as al-Jawbān" (see *K. al-Mubashshirāt*, Yusuf Ağa 5624, fol. 700). This suggests that she was the mother of Ibn ʿArabī's second son, who is more commonly known as Saʿduddīn Muḥammad (b.1221) and was a well-known

said to her: "Do you aspire to the Path?" She said to him: "Yes, by God, I aspire to the Path but I do not know how to reach it." He said: "By means of five things: trust (*tawakkul*), certainty (*yaqīn*), patience (*ṣabr*), resolution (*'azīma*) and veracity (*ṣidq*)." When she told this dream to me, I said to her: "This is the method of the People of God." I will discuss these later in the book, God willing, for they possess specific "doors" (openings, *abwāb*). The four things which we have just mentioned also possess specific doors, which will be described in the second section (*faṣl*) of this book.[13]

"God speaks the Truth and it is He who guides on the way."[14]

---

poet, and that she herself came from an important Seljuk aristocratic family (*khātūn* being the equivalent of princess).

13. The second *faṣl* of the *Futūhāt* concerns proper conduct (*mu'āmalāt*) and contains descriptions of spiritual degrees or stations (*maqām*), usually in opposing, mutually exclusive pairs. Ibn 'Arabī is here referring to the following chapters: seclusion and abandoning seclusion (Chapters 80 and 81); silence and speaking (Chapters 96 and 97); vigilance and sleep (Chapters 98 and 99); hunger and abandoning hunger (Chapters 106 and 107). The same applies to the interior qualities: trust and abandoning trust (Chapters 118 and 119); certainty and abandoning certainty (Chapters 122 and 123); patience and abandoning patience (Chapters 124 and 125); veracity and abandoning veracity (Chapters 136 and 137).

14. Q.33.4.

APPENDIX B

Arabic Text and Manuscripts

This new critical edition of the *Ḥilyat al-abdāl* has been compiled from the oldest manuscripts available, all of which are held in Turkish libraries.

Manuscripts

There are a huge number of surviving manuscripts of the *Ḥilyat al-abdāl* (RG 237), testimony to its enduring popularity. Osman Yahya lists 75 copies spread throughout the world. There are further library copies that Yahya was unaware of (e.g. Milli in Ankara), and probably privately held copies, so the total number of surviving copies is likely to be far more.

The most important manuscript copy is undoubtedly **Yusuf Ağa 4868, pp. 74–83**. On page 83 it states that it was "completed in the protected town of Malatya in the land of Rūm [Anatolia] on the 9th of Rabiʻ al-Awwal 602 (= 24 October 1205).[1] Praise belongs to God, may His praise be confirmed, and may blessings be upon our master Muhammad, His prophet and servant, and upon the elevated ones (*al-āʻlūn*) who come after him." In the margin there is a further note stating that it was checked through reading aloud and certified as correct.

According to Osman Yahia and recent handwriting analysis, the copy is in the hand of Ibn ʻArabī, and it bears all the hallmarks of his writing style. However, there are three lines at the beginning of the text that refer to Ibn ʻArabī as "our master and our

1. That is, over two and a half years after the date of composition in 599/1203.

imam, the shaykh, the imam…" (*sayyidunā wa imāmunā al-shaykh al-imām* etc.). In his other works he invariably refers to himself as "the poor towards God" (*al-faqīr ilā Allāh*). So how are we to account for this peculiar addition to the text, which is not found in any other works? Could it have been added by someone else who was copying his handwriting? Such a thesis is not borne out by the actual manuscript, which is clearly written in the same ink and pen throughout. Is it possible that the analysis of his handwriting is erroneous and that in fact the whole manuscript was written by one of his close disciples with a very similar Maghribi hand? This also seems highly unlikely, as the scribe does not give their name or mention the source of the copy, the writing was done at the very beginning of Ibn ʿArabī's time in Anatolia, and other similar texts in this collection would later become part of Ṣadruddīn al-Qūnawī's private library, that is, bequeathed to him by the author.

Given that the whole treatise including the prefatory addition is in Ibn ʿArabī's hand, we have to look for the explanation within the text itself. Why would Ibn ʿArabī refer to himself in the third person? The clue lies in the nature of the *abdāl*, the transcendent saints who "leave behind his substitute" (p. 83 Arabic): in other words, Ibn ʿArabī is both the scribe who writes the words "our master etc says…" and the real author of the text, the one who receives the inspiration of the treatise and dictates it to himself. He is thus describing his own authorial reality as "the gnostic, the unique, the verifier, the best of the Prophet's own circle and the support of those who follow" (titles which, incidentally, his own students would reiterate in other works). As scribe, he calls his true nature "Reviver of the Religion" (*muḥyī al-dīn*). In short, he is explaining to the reader that he is one of the *abdāl*, one who has clarified the two aspects of his nature, the transcendent and the immanent.

There is one further clue to this reading: near the end of the text, just before the final poem and prayer, he writes: "And regarding this I say" (*wa-fī dhālika qultu*), placing the word *qultu* ("I say") deliberately on its own on one line. Here he switches voices and now writes from the place of the scribe, the faithful servant.[2]

This holograph copy has been used as the primary manuscript for this edition. A further 28 have been consulted, of which the following (in date order) are the most significant:

Milli A571, folios 1b and 166a–168b, copied in Konya in 668 (based on other works), in a clear Seljuk naskhi, partially vowelled. It refers to the author at the beginning as "the master of masters, reviver of the community and the religion" (*shaykh al-mashāyikh muḥyī al-milla wa al-dīn*).

Carulla 986, folios 103b–104a, a very accurate copy probably written pre-700, but there is no indication that it was written during the lifetime of the author as claimed by Yahya.

Veliyuddin 1800, folios 132a–144a, dated 707, copied from a copy of Yusuf Ağa 4868 made by Ibn ʿArabī's close disciple Ayyūb b. Badr al-Muqrī that was checked and certified by the author himself in his house in Damascus in 617. However, despite this pedigree the text has several misreadings and omissions, perhaps due to the difficulty of reading Ayyūb b. Badr's handwriting.

Shehit Ali 1341, folios 148b–150b, dated *c.*724 (based on other works).

Veliyuddin 51, folios 132a–136a, dated 762, copied from Yusuf Ağa 4868.
Fatih 5298, folios 85a–88b, dated 7 Ramaḍān 783.

Shehit Ali 1340, folios 207a–211b, dated *c.*789 (based on other works).

Shehit Ali 1342, folios 202b–204a, dated 837.

2. I owe this explanation to my wife Suha.

Printed editions

The work has also been printed, as part of the *Rasā' il Ibn al-'Arabī*, in Hyderabad (1948), on the basis of Asafiya 376, as well as having innumerable reprintings in the Arab world. From an earlier 1929 edition printed in Damascus, it was first translated into a European language by Michel Vâlsan, who collated the text with two manuscripts in the Bibliothèque Nationale in Paris (*Études Traditionelles*, nos. 286 and 287, 1950, and republished in 1992 by Les Éditions de l'Oeuvre).

BIBLIOGRAPHY

Anṣārī, ʿAbd Allāh. *Ṭabaqāt al-ṣūfiyya*. Tehran, 1983.

Abū Ṭālib al-Makkī. *Qūt al-qulūb*. Cairo, 1961.

Addas, Claude. *Quest for the Red Sulphur*. Cambridge, 1993.

Austin, Ralph. *Sufis of Andalusia*. Sherborne, Gloucestershire, 1988. Partial translation of Ibn ʿArabī's *Rūḥ al-quds* and *Durrat al-fākhira*.

Chittick, William. *The Self-Disclosure of God*. Albany, 1998.

Chodkiewicz, Michel. *Seal of the Saints*. Cambridge, 1993.

— "*Miʿrāj al-kalima*", in *Reason and Inspiration*. Edited Todd Lawson. London, 2005.

Corbin, Henry. *Spiritual Body and Celestial Earth*. Princeton, 1977.

Elmore, Gerald. *Islamic Sainthood in the Fullness of Time*. Leiden, 1999.

al-Ḥabashī. *K. al-Inbāh*. Translated Denis Gril as "The *Kitâb al-inbâh ʿalâ tarîq Allâh* of ʿAbdallah Badr al-Habashi: an account of the spiritual teaching of Muhyiddin Ibn ʿArabi". *Journal of the Muhyiddin Ibn ʿArabi Society*, XV, 1994.

Hirtenstein, Stephen. *The Unlimited Mercifier*. Oxford, 1999.

Ibn ʿArabī. *Divine Sayings (Mishkāt al-anwār)*. Translated Stephen Hirtenstein and Martin Notcutt. Oxford, 2004.

— *al-Futūḥāt al-Makkiyya*. Beirut, n.d.

— *The Meccan Revelations*, Vol. II. New York, 2004.

— *Mawāqiʿ al-nujūm*. Cairo, 1965.

— *La Parure des Abdāl* (*Ḥilyat al-abdāl*). Translated Michel Vâlsan. Paris, 1992.

— *Rasāʾil Ibn al-ʿArabī*. 2 vols. Hyderabad, 1948.

— *Rūḥ al-quds*. Edited Mahmud Ghorab. Damascus, 1986.

— *El Secreto de los Nombres de Dios* (*Kashf al-maʿnā*). Edited and translated Pablo Beneito. Murcia, 1997.

— *The Seven Days of the Heart* (*Awrād*). Translated Pablo Beneito and Stephen Hirtenstein. Oxford, 2000.

— *K. al-Shawāhid*. In *Rasāʾil Ibn al-ʿArabī*. 2 vols. Hyderabad, 1948.

— *Tarjumān al-ashwāq*. Translated Reynold Nicholson. London, 1978.

— *La Vie Merveilleuse de Dhū l-Nūn l'Égyptien*. Translated Roger Deladrière. Paris, 1988.

Ibn ʿAsakir. *al-Taʾrikh al-kabīr*. Damascus, 1911.

Ibn Hanbal. *Musnad*. Beirut, n.d.
Ibn Sawdakīn. *K. al-Wasā' il al-sā' il*. Edited Manfred Profitlich. Freiburg, 1973.
Lane, Edward. *An Arabic-English Lexicon*, in 8 parts. Beirut, 1968.
Smith, Margaret. *An Early Mystic of Baghdad: A Study of the Life and Teaching of Ḥārith b. Asad al-Muḥāsibī*. London, 1935.
Yousef, Mohamed Haj. *Ibn 'Arabî: Time and Cosmology*. Abingdon and New York, 2008.

INDEX OF NAMES AND TERMS

حليةُ الأبْدال

للمحي الدين

ابن العربي

تحقيق: استيفان هيرتنستاين

رموز التحقيق:– Y = يوسف آغا 4868.

– M = ملي A571.

بسم الله الرحمن الرحيم صلى الله على سيدنا محمد واله أجمعين

حِليةُ الأبْدال

وما يظهر عنها من المعارف والاحوال[1]

الحمد لله على ما الْهم، وان علّمنا ما لم نكن نعْلم، و كان فضل الله علينا عظيماً، وصلى الله على السيد الاكْرم، المعطي جوامع الكلم بالموقف الاعْظم، وسلّم تسليماً

امّا بعد

فانّي استخرت الله تعالى ليلة الاثنين الثاني عشر من جمادى الأولى سنة تسع وتسعين وخمس مائه بمنزل آل ميّة بالطايف في زيارتنا عبْد الله بن العباس ابن عم رسول الله صلى الله عليه و سلّم. و كان سبب استخارتي سؤال صاحبيّ ابي محمد عبد الله بدر بن عبد الله الحبشي عتيق ابي الغنايم بن ابي الفتوح الحرّاني رحمه الله وابي

1. Y+: قال سيدنا وامامنا الشيخ الامام العارف الاوحد المحقق بقية السلف وعمرة الخلف محى الدين ابو عبد الله محمد بن على ابن محمد ابن العربي الطائى الحاتمى الاندلسي رضى الله عنه.
M+: هذه رساله من تصانف شيخ المشائخ محى المله والدين رضى الله عنه وارضاه.

عبد الله محمد بن خالد الصدفي التلمساني وفقهما الله ان اقيّد لهما في هذه الايام ايام الزيارة ما ينْتفعون به في طريق الاخرة.

فاستخرتُ الله في ذلك وقيدْت لهما هذه الكراسة التي وسمتُها حلية الابدال وما يظهر عنها من المعارف والاحوال، تكون لهما ولغيرهما عوْناً على طريق السعادة وباباً جامعاً لفنون الارادة. ومن مُوجِدِ الكون نسأل التأييد والعون.

فصل

الحُكم نتيجة الحِكمة والعلم نتيجة المعرفة. فمن لا حكمة له لا حكم له، ومن لا معرفة له لا علم له. فالحاكم العالم لله قائم، والحكيم العارف بالله واقف. فالحاكمون العالمون لاميون والحكماء العارفون بائيون.

لما شُغِف الزاهد بترك دنياه والمتوكل بكِلَته امره الى مولاه، والمريد بالسماع والوجد والعابد بالعبادة والجهد والحكيم العارف بالهمّة والقصد، غاب العالمون الحاكمون في الغيب، فلم يعرفهم عارفٌ ولا

مريد ولا عابدٌ ولا شهدهم متوكل ولا زاهدٌ. فترك الزاهد للعِوَض ووكل المتوكل لنيل الغرض، وتواجد المريد لتنفيس الكرب واجتهد العابد رغبةً في القرب، وقصد العارف الحكيم بهمته الوصول، وانما يتجلّى الحق لمن امّحى رسْمُه وزال عنه اسْمُه.

فالمعرفة حجابٌ على المعروف، والحكمة بابٌ عنده يكون الوقوف، وما بقي من الاوصاف فاسباب كالحروف. وهذه كلّها علل تعْمي الابصار وتطمِس الانوار. فلولا وجود الكون لظهر العين، ولولا الاسماء لبرز المسمَّى، ولولا المحبّة لاستمرّ الوصال، ولولا الحظوظ لمُلِكت المراتب، ولولا الهوية لظهرتْ الانية، ولولا هو لكان، ولولا انت لبدا رَسْم الجهْل قائماً، ولولا الفهْم لقوي سلطان العلْم. فاذا تلاشت هذه الظُلَم، و طارت بمرهفات الفناء هذه البُهَم

تجلّى لقلبك من لم يزل به قاطناً في غيوب الازل
وما حجب العين عن دركها سواك ولاكن بضرب المثل
تبيّن للقلب انّ الذي رآه به دايما لم يزل
وجاء خطاب يعمّ الكلام ويبدي سناه رسوم المحلّ

فصل

كان لنا بمرْشانة الزيتون ببلاد الاندلس صاحبٌ من الصالحين يعلّم القرآن وكان فقيهاً مجيداً حافظاً ذا وَرَع وفضلٍ وخدمة للفقراء، اسمه عبد المجيد بن سلمة. واخبرني وفقه الله قال بيْنا انا ليلةً في مُصلاّي قد اكملت حزبي وجعلت رأسي بين ركبتيّ اذكرالله اذ تحسّست بشخصٍ قد نفض مصلاّي من تحتي وبسط عوضاً منه حَصير خصفٍ وقال صلّ عليه وباب بيتي عليّ مغلق. فداخلني منه جزعٌ فقال لي: من تآنس بالله لم يجزع. ثم قال لي: اتق الله في كل حالٍ. ثم انّي الهمْتُ فقلت له: يا سيدي بماذا يصير الابدال ابدالاً؟ فقال لي: بالاربعة التي ذكرها ابو طالب في القوت، الصمت والعزلة والجوع والسهر. ثم انصرف عنّي ولا اعرف كيف دخل ولا كيف خرج غير ان بابي على حاله مغلق والحصير الذي اعطانيه تحتي.

وهذا الرجل فهو من الابدال واسمه معاذ بن اشرَس رضي الله عنه.

فهذه الاربع التي ذكرها فهي عماد هذا الطريق الاسْنى وقوائمه، ومن

لا قدم له فيها ولا رسوخ فهو تائهٌ عن طريق الله تعالى. وغرضنا في هذه الكراسة الكلام في هذه الفصول الاربعة وما تعطيه من المعارف والاحوال. جعلنا الله واياكم ممن تحقّق بها وداوم عليها انّه على ذلك قدير.

فصل في الصَمْت

الصمت على قسمين: صمتٌ باللسان عن الحديث بغير الله تعالى مع غير الله تعالى جملةً واحدةً، وصمت بالقلب عن خاطرٍ يخطرُ له في النفس في كون من الاكوان البتّة. فمن صمت لسانه ولم يصمت قلبه خف وزره، ومن صمت لسانه وقلبه ظهر له سرّه وتجلّى له ربّه، ومن صمت قلبه ولم يصمت لسانه فهو ناطق بلسان الحكمة، ومن لم يصْمت بلسانه ولا بقلبه كان مملكةً للشيطان ومسخرةً له.

فصمت اللسان من منازل العامّة وارباب السلوك، وصمت القلب من صفات المقرّبين اهل المشاهدات .وحال صمت السالكين السلامة من الآفات، وحال صمت المقرّبين مخاطبات التأنيس. فمن التزم الصمت

من جميع الاحْوال كلّها لم يبق له حديثُ الا مع ربّه. فانّ الصمت على الانسان مُحال في نفسه فاذا انتقل من الحديث مع الاغيار الى الحديث مع ربّه كان نجياً مقرّباً مؤيداً في نطقه اذا نطق بالصواب لانّه ينطقِ عن الله. قال تعالى في حقّ نبيه عليه السلام: وما ينطق عن الهوى. فالنطق بالصواب نتيجة الصمت عن الخطاء. والكلام مع غير الله خطأ بكل حال، وبغير الله شرّ من كل وجْه. قال تعالى: لا خيْرَ في كثيرٍ من نجْواهم الا من أمر بصدقةٍ او معروفٍ او اصْلاحٍ بين الناس بكمال شروطها. قال الله تعالى: وما امروا الا ليعبدوا الله مخلصين له الدين. ولحال الصمت مقام الوحي على ضروبه. والصمت يورث معرفة الله تعالى.

فصل في العُزْلَة

العزلة سبب لصمت الانسان فمن اعتزل عن الناس لم يجد من يحادثه فادّاه ذلك الى الصمت باللسان. والعزلة على قسمين: عزلة المريدين وهي بالاجسام عن مخالطة الاغيار وعزلة المحقّقين وهي بالقلوب عن

الاكوان فليست قلوبهم مجالاً لشيئ سوى العلم بالله تعالى الذي هو شاهد الحق فيها الحاصل من المشاهدة.

وللمعتزلين نيات ثلاث نيّة اتقاء شرّ الناس ونيّة اتقاء شرّه المتعدّي الى الغير وهو ارفع من الاول فان في الاول سوء الظنّ بالناس وفي الثاني سوء الظنّ بنفسه وسوء الظنّ بنفسك اولى لانّك بنفسك اعرف. ونيّة ايثار صحبة المولى من جانب الملأ الاعلى فأعْلى الناس من اعتزل عن نفسه ايثاراً لصحبة ربه فمن آثر العزلة على المخالطة فقد آثر ربّه على غيره ومن آثر ربّه لم يعرف احدٌ ما يعْطيه الله تعالى من المواهب و الاسرار. ولا تقع العزلة ابداً في القلب الا من وحْشة تطرأ على القلب من المعْتزَل عنه وانس بالمعْتزَل اليه وهو الذي يسُوقه الى العزلة.

وكانت العزلة تغْني عن شرط الصمت فانّ الصمت لازمٌ لها فهذا صمت اللسان. وامّا صمت القلب فلا تعْطيه العزلة فقد يتحدّث الواحد في نفسه بغير الله تعالى مع غير الله تعالى فلهذا جعلنا الصمت ركناً

من الاركان في الطريق قائماً بنفسه.

فمن لازم العزلة وقف على سرّ الوحدانية الإلاهية هذا ينتج له من المعارف ومن الاسرار اسرار الاحدية التي هي الصفة. وحال العزلة التنزيه عن الاوْصاف سالكاً كان المعتزل او محقّقاً. وارفع احْوال العزلة الخلوة فانّ الخلوة عزلةٌ في العزلة فنتيجتها اقوى من نتيجة العزلة العامّة. فينبغي للمعْتزل ان يكونَ صاحب يقين مع الله تعالى حتى لا يكونَ له خاطرٌ متعلّقُ خارجاً عن بيت عزلته فان حرم اليقين فليستعدّ لعزلته قوته زمان عزلته حتى يتقوى يقينُه بما يتجلّى له في عزلته لابدّ من ذلك هذا شرط محكمٌ من شروط العزلة. والعزلة تورث معرفة الدنْيا.

فصل في الجُوْع

الجوع هو الركن الثالث من اركان هذا الطريق الإلاهي. وهو يتضمّن الركن الرابع الذي هو السَهَر كالعزلة تتضمن الصمت. والجوع جوعا: جوع اختيارٍ وهو جوع السالكين، وجوع اضطرارٍ وهو جوع

المحقّقين. فان المحقّق لا يجوّع نفسه ولكن قد يَقلل اكْله ان كان في مقام الانْس. فان كان في مقام الهيبة كثر اكله فكثرة الاكل للمحقّقين دليل على صحّة سطوات انوار الحقيقة على قلوبهم بحال العَظمة من مشهودهم. وقلّة الاكل دليل على صحّة المحادثة بحال المؤانسة من مشهودهم. وكثرة الاكل للسالكين دليل على بعدهم من الله تعالى وطرْدهم عن بابه واستيلاء النفس الشهوانية البهيمية بسلطانها عليهم. وقلّة الاكل لهم دليل على نفحات الجود الإلاهي على قلوبهم فيشغلهم ذلك عن تدبير جسومهم.

والجوع بكل حال ووَجْهٍ سببُ دَاع للسالك والمحقّق الى نيل عظيم الاحْوال للسالكين والاسْرار للمحقّقين. ما لم يفرط بضجرٍ من الجائع فانّه اذا افرط ادّى الى الهوَس وذهاب العقل وفساد المزاج فلا سبيل للسالك ان يجوع الجوع المطلوب لنيْل الاحْوال الا عن امر شيخ. وامّا وَحْده فلا سبيل لكن يتعيّن على السالك اذا كان وَحْده التقليل من الطعام واستدامة الصيام ولزوم اكلةٍ واحدة بين الليل والنهار وان

يغبّ بالإدام الدسم فلا يأتدم في الجمعة سوَى مرّتين ان اراد ان ينتفع حتى يجدَ شيخاً فاذا وَجَده سلّم امره اليه وشيخه يدبّر حاله وامره اذ الشيخ اعْرف بمصالحه منه.

وللجوع حالُ ومقامُ، فحاله الخشوع والخضوع والمسْكنة والذلّة والافتقار وعدم الفضول و سكون الجوارح وعدم الخواطر الردية، هذا حال الجوع للسالكين. وامّا حاله في المحقّقين فالرقّة و الصفاء والمؤانسة وذهاب الكون والتنزّه عن اوْصاف البشرية بالعزّة الإلاهية والسلطان الربّاني. ومقامه المقام الصمداني وهو مقامُ عالٍ له اسرارُ وتجلّيات واحوال، ذكرناها في كتاب مواقع النجوم في عُضْو القلب منه ولكن في بعض النسخ فاني استدركته فيه بمدينة بجاية سنة سبع وتسعين وخمس مائة، وكان قد خرجتْ منه نسخٌ كثيرة في البلاد لم يثبت فيها هذا المنزل. فهذا فائدة الجوع المصاحب للهمّة لا جوع العامّة، فان جوع العامّة جوع صلاح المزاج وتنْعيم البدن بالصحّة لا غير. والجوع يورث معرفة الشيطان عصمنا الله واياكم منه.

فصل في السَهَر

السهر نتيجة الجوع. فانّ المعْدة اذا لم يكن فيها طعامٌ ذهب النوم. والسهر سهران: سهر العين وسهر القلب. فسهر القلب انتباهُه من نومات الغفلات طلباً للمشاهدات، وسهر العين رغبة في بقاء الهمّة في القلب لطلب المسامرة. فانّ العين اذا نامتْ بطل عمل القلب فانْ كان القلب غير نائمٍ مع نوم العين فغايته مشاهدة سهره المتقدّم لا غير. وامّا ان يلحظ غير ذلك فلا. ففايدة السهر استمرار عمل القلب وارتقاء المنازل العلية المخزونة عند الله تعالى.

وحال السهر تعْمير الوقت خاصّة للسالك والمحقّق، غير انّ المحقّق في حاله زيادة تخلّق ربّاني لا يعرفُه السالك. وامّا مقامه فمقام القيّومية. وربّما بعض اصحابنا منع ان يتحقّق احدُ بالقيّومية وبعضهم منع من التخلّق بها. لقيتُ ابا عبد الله بن جنيد فوجدْته يمنع من ذلك، وامّا نحن فلا نقول بذلك فقد اعطتنا الحقايق انّ الانسان الكامل لا يبقى له في الحضرة الإلاهية اسم الا وهو حامل له. ومن

توقف من اصحابنا في مثل هذه المسْألة فلعدم معرفته بما هو الانسان عليه في حقيقته ونشأته، فلو عرف نفسه ما عسُر عليه مثل هذا. والسهر يورث معرفة النفس.

وتمّت اركان المعرفة اذ المعرفة تدورُ على تحصيل هذه الاربعة المعارف، معرفة الله والنفس والدنيا والشيطان. فاذا اعْتزل الانسان عن الخلق وعن نفسه وصمت عن ذكره بذكر ربّه اياه واعْرض عن الغِذاء الجسماني وسهر عند موافقة نوم النائمين واجتمعتْ فيه هذه الخصال الاربعة، بُدّلتْ بشريته مَلكاً وعبوديته سيادةً وعقله حسّاً وغيبه شهادةً وباطنه ظاهراً.

واذا رحل عن موضع ترك بدله فيه حقيقة روحانية يجتمع اليها ارواح اهل ذلك الموطن الذي رحل عنه هذا الولي. فانْ ظهر شوقٌ من اناسي ذلك الموطن شديدٌ لهذا الشخص تجسّدتْ لهم تلك الحقيقة الروحانية التي تركها بدله فكلّمها وكلّمتْه وهو يتخيل انه مطلوبه وهو غائبٌ عنه حتى يقضي حاجته منه. وقد تتجسّد هذه الروحانية ان كان

من صاحبها شوق اوْ تعلّق همّة بذلك الموطن. وقد يكون هذا مَن غير البدل. والفرق بينهما انّ البدل يرحل ويعلم انّه ترك بدله، وغير البدل لا يعْرف ذلك وان تركه، لانّه لم يحكم هذه الاربعة الاركان التي ذكرناها. وفي ذلك قلت

يا منْ اراد منازل الابدال	من غير قصدْ ٍمنه للاعمال
لا تطمعنّ بها فلست من اهلها	ان لم تزاحمهم على الاحوال
واصمتْ بقلبك واعتزل عن كل مَن	يُدْنيك من غير الحبيب الوالي
واذا سهرت وجعْت نلتَ مقامهم	وصحبتهم في الحلّ والترْحال
بيت الولاية قسّمت اركْانه	ساداتنا فيه من الابدال
ما بيْن صمت واعتزال دائمٍ	والجوع والسهرالنزيه العالي

والله يوفّقنا واياكم لاستعمال هذه الاركان وينزّلنا واياكم منازل الاحسان انّه الولي المنان.[2]

2. Y+: تمت الكراسة بمحروسه ملطيه في بلاد الروم في التاسع من شهر ربيع الاول سنة اثنين وستمايه والحمد لله حق حمده والصلاة على سيدنا محمد نبيه وعبده والاعلون من بعده. بلغ سماعا ومقابلة.

Ḥilyat al-abdāl wa mā yaẓharu ʿanhā min al-maʿārif wa al-aḥwāl

Muḥyī al-dīn Muḥammad
b. ʿAlī b. al-ʿArabī

Arabic text by Stephen Hirtenstein

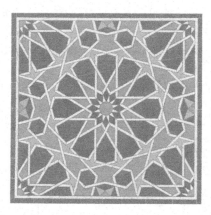